THOMAS KINKADE
Painter of Light™

Heart
Reflections

Devotional
Companion for the
Reflections from
the Heart of God Bible

HEART REFLECTIONS BY
Nanette Kinkade

THOMAS NELSON PUBLISHERS
Nashville

Heart Reflections

Dear Sisters in Christ,

We are so excited that you are here! Nanette and I have prayed that through this devotional book you would catch a glimpse of God's beautiful love for you. I constantly stand amazed at the vastness of God's power, the intricate beauty of His creativity, the boundless depths of His love. It is my prayer that you will stand in awe with us as we take His Word—His heart—to ours, and allow it to change our lives forever.

I echo Thom's enthusiasm, but with a little trepidation. In the following pages you will find our hearts, our home, exposed as never before. My walk with God is not without flaws—but it is full of His grace. I pray that as you peruse these scriptures and devotionals you will understand we are all "a work in progress," and that we have an incredible God who is faithful to accomplish all that He desires in our lives when we surrender to Him.

In one of these devotionals, I mention my personal "tea time with Jesus." My prayer is that you will find your own precious time with the Savior, and that God's Word along with this devotional book will help you enter into a profoundly personal relationship with Him. Reflect on His goodness. Record what you learn. And revel in His love for you.

We welcome you—and so does He.

Thom and Nanette Kinkade

Contents

Rest and Receive

Put down your pens and pencils. Put aside your mental checklists. The following pages are not for you to do. They are for you to receive, and to be. It is not that Christianity is a system of beliefs without actions. James warns us strongly that our behavior clearly illustrates our beliefs. But I do believe that the biggest battleground for Christians begins in the mind, where the Word of God wages war against our sinful selves and the sinister plans of Satan who longs to see God's children deluded out of the riches of Christ that are rightfully theirs. It is so easy for Christians to emphasize activity because activity exists in the realm of the tangible, observable, and quantifiable. We can count conversions, number our devotions, chalk up our charities, and secretly hope that the tally proves our worthiness to receive God's love and attention. But as He says throughout His Word, God cares about our hearts and right motives more than our resumé.

Knowing God begins with knowing He is God. Christ's atoning work for you alone makes you worthy to approach His throne to learn from Him. Inherently, resting means to rely on His righteousness. If our relationship with God feels anything other than restful, it is likely that we are injecting our own agenda or working through the motions of worship without ever truly entering God's presence. True worship requires truth in your inner being, fully exposed before the eyes of God where you and He meet together in intimate union. It is your special place with God, your sanctuary where your soul is refreshed with living water, your sins are wiped clean, and your spirit is ignited by the passion of His love.

Now is the time for true worship. Works will flow from the power He Himself will give you. God is calling you. So put all else aside and sit at His feet. Rest and receive from Him the love and power He longs to lavish on you, His chosen child.

Heart Matters

*For I desire mercy and not sacrifice, and the knowledge of God
more than burnt offerings.*

HOSEA 6:6

If self-confidence and optimism could attain heaven, I
was a shoe-in. If other people's opinion of me and my
own dedication to living life in its fullest were required
for God's approval, my resumé was full. As I saw it, I did
have it together, though deep inside of my heart an
aching for intimacy I did not know with God lay quietly
like a dormant seed. And just as the Scripture says a seed
must die to yield its fruit, so God had His way in me to
produce the life of Christ.

I believe that is one of the reasons God allowed me to
break my leg so badly. I actually needed to break—not
just physically, but spiritually as well—from all the
things in which I had placed my hope.

It is a frightening place to be fully broken before God. All
pretenses gone, it is just He and I and the ugly truth—
my sinfulness. But when I came before Him openly and
honestly an interesting thing happened. He didn't accuse

me of wasted years away from Him. He didn't tell me to get my act together first. He didn't even say He felt sorry for me, or that I deserved His attention. What He did tell me was that He loved me, and He had been waiting all those years just for me to come to Him.

One day after my prayer to God, Thom—now my husband—called me out of the blue to ask me out on a date. Though we hadn't seen each other in a year, Thom shared the gospel of Christ with me that night, and I gave my heart to Him. At my weakest moment, I found my greatest strength—Christ Himself. It was a miraculous beginning in grace, and it is through that same grace that I daily realize God's faithful favor and rejoice in His abundant love that is forever mine.

Dear Heavenly Father,
Thank You for Your Son Jesus Christ. Thank You that He alone makes me worthy to stand before Your throne. Forgive me, Father, for my futile attempts to earn Your approval, to try to prove my own righteousness apart from You. I know that in Your Son I have Your full favor because You see His righteousness, not my sin. And since You desire it, help me most of all to know You better.

Heart Reflections

BUILDING FAMILIES OF FAITH

In your own words, what is

God saying in Hosea 6:6?

In what ways do you rely on your own strength or goodness instead of turning to God?

Name some specific ways you can tear down religious pretenses in your own life and cultivate an open and honest relationship with God.

Hide and Seek

Then you will call upon Me and go and pray to Me, and I will listen to you. And you will seek Me and find Me, when you search for Me with all your heart.

JEREMIAH 29:12, 13

With four girls and a husband with an overloaded schedule, finding time to be alone is not easy. True quiet time is a rare and precious necessity I need to refocus, rethink, and remember the sovereignty of God in the midst of my busy day. Right now my quiet time falls in mid-afternoon. Evie's napping and the others are at school, so I indulge in what is one of my most favorite luxuries—tea time with Jesus.

It starts with a freshly brewed cup of peppermint tea. Like a date, I meet with Jesus during this special time where I talk to Him and sit quietly as I listen for His voice. Phones are unanswered. All radios are off. Nothing from the outside world distracts. It is an intensely intimate moment with my Savior, the Creator of the world, meeting with me in my humble living room. Suddenly the stresses of the day fade away in the glory of

His presence. Renewed perspective and a refreshed soul refuel my tank so that I can then face whatever comes my way, knowing the same Spirit of God I knew in the quiet is still present with me in the midst of life's chaos.

Dear sisters in Christ, it is not impossible to find this time. Remember that with God all things are possible. And this time—it is soul time for you, a requisite pleasure you must have to continue to give of yourself to so many, as you already do. It is not a replacement for Bible study, for that is necessary to stay grounded in the truth. But it is the supplement that takes head knowledge to heart, and harbors that deeply personal relationship with God that you so long to have.

Dear Jesus,
What a blessing it is to find You, know You, and hear You in
the midst of the day. You are a God of details, and I am
grateful that You are interested in all the minute details of my
life. I welcome You, Holy Spirit, to come and teach me how to
hear Your voice. Help me to find the right time for You and I
to meet, and once there, to draw on You for comfort, wisdom,
and strength.

Heart Reflections

BUILDING FAMILIES OF FAITH

What distracts you from
spending time with God?

*How does Scripture reading
and prayer better equip you to
face the day?*

*What are some ways you can
rearrange your schedule/
priorities to find time alone
with Him?*

*Is there someone you know who
could help encourage you in this
endeavor? How?*

Interior Decorating

Do not let your adornment be merely outward—arranging the hair, wearing gold, or putting on fine apparel—rather let it be the hidden person of the heart, with the incorruptible beauty of a gentle and quiet spirit, which is very precious in the sight of God.

1 PETER 3:3, 4

She was sitting just a few feet away from my girls, and I was afraid of what they might say. Her face was shriveled and shrunken from life's many years of wear and tear. Her washed-out face paled only to the powder-white, thinning hair above. Her limbs looked as feeble as chalk. But though the outside was wasting away, a curious warmth of life shone from her eyes. She was old, but not gone. She was fragile in frame, but still strong in Christ—and she encouraged my girls to be so, too.

It was one of life's precious moments, the kind I pray God will bring the way of my girls more often. It is the opportunity to see God's version of beauty—a gentle and quiet spirit—wrought in the furnace of life over the course of many years.

That kind of beauty doesn't happen overnight. It is a process of daily surrendering your desires, your will, and your thoughts to the Lord, allowing His Word to redesign your heart from the inside out. As His character comes out through us, a beautiful transformation takes place. Sure, you may still have that nose that sticks out too long, or legs too short, or a bulging mid-section that won't seem to go away. But an inner beauty emerges that attracts others on a spiritual level, opening the door to evangelism in ways we would never have otherwise. God warns us again and again in His Word that physical beauty is fleeting. We are like grass in the field that springs up, only to wither and die. But what lasts forever is Christ in us, our hope of glory. The beauty found in Him never fades away.

Father,

Time and again You have told Your children that what matters to You is the condition of our hearts. I worry so much about how I appear to others on the outside that I sometimes fail to see the significance of inner beauty, and I repent. I want to not only see myself as You see me—God's child clothed in Christ's robe of righteousness—but I also want to see the inner beauty of others through Your eyes of love.

Heart Reflections

BUILDING FAMILIES OF FAITH

Why do you think the world is

obsessed with physical beauty?

What qualities does God say
makes a person beautiful?

Take an inventory of your
incoming stimulus. Is there
anything that serves as a
stumbling block to you—
focusing your attention on
externals instead of internals?

How can you cultivate inner
character in yourself and in
your children?

Righting Wrongs

Therefore if you bring your gift to the altar, and there remember that your brother has something against you, leave your gift there before the altar, and go your way. First be reconciled to your brother, and then come and offer your gift.

MATTHEW 5:23, 24

Sometimes you can almost touch the tension. A whole house full of girls—each with their own agenda—can be a breeding ground for disgruntled relationships. And for every moment the issue goes unaddressed, the attitudes become all the more sour. So what of my plans to teach the girls about God? To play Christian music in the house? To take them on trips to share the gospel with others? It must wait. The urgent priority now is restored relationships. Repentance. Forgiveness.

At first it may seem forced. Mom is making them do this. But as the words come out of their mouths, "I was wrong. Will you forgive me?" the spirit of ugliness is released, making room for Christ's light to shine once again. They seal the deal with an embrace, a physical gesture of harmony that inevitably sends the girls back to giggling and rejoicing in their relationships. Now we can get on with our walk with God.

We can learn a lot from children because adult problems aren't so far removed. In our spiritual family we must keep the same level of honesty and forgiveness that are required in a tightly knit home. It may seem difficult or contrived at first to confront someone we have wronged or someone who has wronged us. But as we develop this pattern of relating, our relationship with Christ will be strengthened, and the body of Christ will be freed to shine His unblemished love to a world who is dying to see it.

Father,
So often I want to walk ahead in the Spirit without dealing
first with the dirtiness of my flesh. My own selfish ambition
and self-centered thinking has muddied the picture of love and
harmony the body of Christ was designed to paint for the
world. Please give me the strength, wisdom, and courage I need
to be vulnerable, penitent, and gracious to your coheirs of
grace. Change my heart so that this pattern of relating
that You have described in Your Word would become
first nature to me.

Heart Reflections

BUILDING FAMILIES OF FAITH

Why is it so difficult to either admit we are wrong, or when wronged, to initiate the reconciliation process?

Why is it important that we
surrender our right to be right
and instead work toward
restoration?

How does our knowledge of
Christ lead us down the path
of forgiveness?

Is there a relationship in your
life that needs to be righted?
What has God called you to do
about it?

Holy Hostages

Finally, brethren, whatever things are true, whatever things are noble, whatever things are just, whatever things are pure, whatever things are lovely, whatever things are of good report, if there is any virtue and if there is anything praiseworthy— meditate on these things.

PHILIPPIANS 4:8

Love your enemies. Pray for those who curse you. Turn the other cheek. Go the extra mile. To the natural mind, God's instructions don't make much sense. In fact, nothing to which Christ calls us comes naturally because sin is our first nature. Anything good we do comes only by His Spirit in us.

That is why we cannot rely on our own power of reasoning to win the battle of our minds. Just as Jesus battled Satan in the wilderness by quoting the Word of God, so we must know Scripture well enough to ward off the Enemy's missiles and proactively take command of our thoughts—the breeding ground for action. According to 2 Corinthians 10:4, 5, we are equipped to take every thought captive and actually make it—force it, if necessary—to be obedient to Christ.

To help our family win the fight, we stick God's Word where we'll see it most—the refrigerator! Little yellow stickies bearing verses from the morning's Bible study adorn the front so that, every time we go to get fed physically, our minds are filled spiritually, too. Praise music is another excellent way to maintain a heavenly focus, even in the midst of a hectic day at home or on the road. Our girls go to sleep listening to Scripture songs, and I unwind with my favorite hand-scripted and drawn book of Psalms. They are small steps to be sure. But each one packs the power of God's inspired Word that, moment by moment, dismantles the Enemy's lies and builds a refuge of faith around our family.

Father,

With thousands of thoughts filling my mind each day, it is easy to lose spiritual ground. But through Your Word, Lord, I can take thoughts captive and win the battle of my mind. I ask You to fill me with Your Holy Spirit, and sensitize my own spirit to You in such a way that I remember Your Word in the time of need. Help me to use it to tear down the strongholds of doubt Satan longs to build in my heart and mind. Protect me from the Evil One, and protect me also from my own deception. Help me to think on those things that best please You.

Heart Reflections

BUILDING FAMILIES OF FAITH

Think for a moment and record the topics that tend to dominate your thought life.

*Are these thoughts honoring to
God?*

*What ways will you combat
Satan's lies and distractions
and hold fast to the Word of
Truth?*

*What Bible verses would you
like to commit to memory this
week to help you win the fight?*

Bulldozing Barriers

The sacrifices of God are a broken spirit, a broken and a contrite heart—these, O God, You will not despise.

PSALM 51:17

Your week could have looked like this: You've gotten up at least one hour before the kids each morning, just to have your quiet time. You've listened to that Christian CD so much you're singing it in your sleep. You've prayed, you've witnessed, and you were present at every Bible study your church offered.

Or it could have been more like this: You overslept your alarm again and missed your appointment with God—for the fifth day in a row. Your kids have been fighting and, tired from a long day, you lose it. Time is wasted on too much TV and, to top it all, you finished off the entire carton of your favorite rocky road ice cream.

Who is ready to approach God's throne? Who has God been waiting to see? Both! The bottom line is that God loves His children. He knows our failings far better than we. We don't approach His throne when we feel like we have lived good enough to receive His grace, because *no one is good enough.* Everyone needs His grace, and there is plenty of it for those who come before Him with a broken and contrite heart.

So no matter what kind of day, days, or lifelong past you've had, be bold to confess your sins to the Lord. He knows them anyway, and He stands ready to wash you clean. Let go of the urge to prove your worthiness. Rest instead in the righteousness of Christ and humbly let Him have His way in your heart.

Dear Father,

Thank You so much for Your unconditional love. Thank You that I do not have to earn Your approval before I enter Your throne room. In Christ, I realize I have Your full favor. In Your perfect love my fear fades away, and I can face the reality of my sin, knowing that my Savior has paid the price in full. Cleanse and renew me, Father, and help me to remember that it was Your grace that saved me, and it is Your grace that will lead me home.

Heart Reflections

BUILDING FAMILIES OF FAITH

In what ways do you sometimes feel you have failed God?

What does God require from
you according to Psalm 51:17
and what does it mean?

When is the best time to
approach God's throne for
mercy?

Who alone makes us worthy?

Royal Quest

But seek first the kingdom of God and His righteousness, and all these things shall be added to you.

MATTHEW 6:33

Success—as the world defines it—has not always been a part of our story. Thom remembers times when his family could hardly find food to eat. My family, though better off financially than Thom's, planned every penny spent, and purchases were always made from the more practical perspective. Though they were stringent times, they have helped us as Thom and I have forged these two family backgrounds now into one. Our pasts help us realize that our possessions don't define us; our desires do.

That's why God says, "Where your treasure is, there your heart will be also" (Matt. 6:21). If we want our hearts to be wholly His, we have to be willing to want what He wants, whatever that is. To help eliminate worldly distractions, our family has taken what some may consider to be drastic measures: no television in the home; no newspapers or women's magazines; simply put, no input at all from media and other worldly sources that contradict God's established values. The pull of the world is too strong, and eliminating the source of distraction simplifies the fight.

Such exercises may or may not be necessary for your family. The Holy Spirit is faithful to lead each of us in the path of righteousness. But where the paths may be different, the goal for all of God's children is the same: to attain Christ, our hope of glory. Everything else pales in comparison. So if anything gets in the way of your pursuit of Him, put it aside. Passionately pursue the pleasure of knowing Him—of seeing His heavenly kingdom—and watch how He faithfully fulfills all of your earthly needs.

Dear Father,
I sometimes find it difficult to be in the world, but not of it.
Because I know that You are faithful and good, I look to You
alone for comfort and for my soul's satisfaction. Only in You
can my deepest desires be met. Please guide my family as we
seek Your kingdom first, and as we look expectantly for You to
fulfill all of our needs.

Heart Reflections

BUILDING FAMILIES OF FAITH

Considering your time and energy, where are most of your efforts spent?

What does it mean to seek
God's kingdom first?

What will God provide if we
seek Him?

What are some practical ways
to put worldly pursuits behind
us and focus instead on
treasures in heaven?

Perfect Peace

And let the peace of God rule in your hearts, to which also you were called in one body; and be thankful.

It was all we had known, and it was what they loved. Our two oldest girls, Merritt and Chandler, had attended a well-respected, private Christian school since their school days began. The other two were soon to enter when the red banners began waving their warnings. Spiritual flags unfurled by the Holy Spirit before my eyes and Thom's signaled that something was amiss and needed our attention. Through weeks of agonizing prayer and discussion, we realized that God had removed His peace in our hearts about our children's school attendance. Instead, He was calling us to move the classroom into our own home, where we could better control the spiritual influences that came into our daughters' lives.

To us, it was a radical move out of a very comfortable place into one that was at best unsure. But as His Word says, "He who calls you is faithful, who also will do it"

(1 Thess. 5:24). Within a year's time, we watched as God worked in our family, bringing a harmony we had never before experienced. Renewed enthusiasm and excitement filled our home, and even test scores (which were already good) increased an incredible 25 percent. It was simply God's confirmation that we had heard, and heeded, the right voice.

It is the blessed privilege of every Christian to walk according to the direction of the Holy Spirit. If we are quiet before Him, and listen, we can often hear His gentle voice guiding us down the right path—a direction that always agrees with the written Word and leads us closer to Him.

Dear Father,
I am so thankful that I have an all-knowing, all-powerful God
to lead and guide me. I rejoice in the gift of life You've given
me—Your Holy Spirit—who is ever helping me find Your face
through His gentle, quiet words of wisdom. Help me to be
sensitive to the sense of peace that comes from walking rightly
with You. And when I can't find it, help me to be patient to
wait on You for direction.

Heart Reflections

BUILDING FAMILIES OF FAITH

Have you ever had a time in
your life where Christ's peace
led your decision making?

How did you see God's
faithfulness in that situation?

What can we do (what are our
resources) if we don't sense His
peace or direction?

Record your prayer to the Holy
Spirit asking Him to clearly
guide you in truth today and
every day.

Cease Striving

Be still, and know that I am God; I will be exalted among the
nations, I will be exalted in the earth!

PSALM 46:10

The sun is just now peeking through the cracks in the shade. I hear the first few birds, heralding the new day's dawn. My eyes are closed, but my mind is at work.

It is here, in the quiet calm before the day's hustle and bustle begins, that we give the day to God. Before our feet even touch the floor, we have met with our Maker in our own minds, handing over to Him each event that the coming day holds. It is a moment of transcendent peace that floods our souls and keeps us singing the rest of the day through.

Do you feel stressed? Are life's worries warping your joy? Are you in such a hurry that you've lost sight of what's most important? Then stop. Be still. In the silence, seek Him. Know Him. Know that He alone controls every moment of your day. He ordains all the challenges you will face. And He holds the solution: Himself. As you sit at His feet, feel the weight of the world lift from your shoulders. Let His love rain down and nourish the parched places of your soul. Then rejoice in song because He has set you free. He will be exalted among the nations, among your family members, and in your heart. He will be exalted in the earth!

Father,

I praise You because You alone are worthy of praise. When I am still, I remember You—that You are the great I AM, who was there for Abraham and Moses, and You are still there for me. What a privilege to know You. Even greater still to be known by You. Help me to see Your hand in the details. And when life seems to be out of control, help me to remember the quiet times, and to know that You have been and always will be Lord of all.

Heart Reflections

BUILDING FAMILIES OF FAITH

What worries weigh you down the most?

How can simply being still and
acknowledging God help free
you from your burden?

What are some ways your soul
can be still, even when chaos is
swirling around you?

What are some verses you can
memorize to remind you of
God's love and sovereignty?

Building Families of Faith

The trumpets sound. The crowd rises and turns. Behold, the bride arrayed in simple, white elegance stands for a moment suspended in time. Before everyone's eyes she transitions from girl to woman as she fixes her gaze ahead on her prize—her mate for life—waiting at the end of the walk. It is one of those few times in life where we get a glimpse of the incredible bond our heavenly Husband, Jesus Christ, feels for His bride, the church. The profundity of the promise is undeniable. It transcends ceremony and soars on supernatural wings before the very throne of God. A covenant is made. New life begins.

But where does this new life go from here? According to statistics, more than half of American marriages dissolve in divorce. Abuse is rampant, and more children than ever before are growing up without fathers, without family, and without a framework for avoiding the same failures themselves. It is easy for some to blame the institution—that marriage itself is the making for disaster. That two different people could never realistically make it together as "one." Truly, for the world, their rationale is not so wrong. Apart from Christ a good marriage in God's eyes is impossible. Empty thrones are soon crowned with self. And self-centered living is love's primary divider.

God's way is different for His children. Submission to each other stems from a surrendered heart to the Father's leading. Marriage simply facilitates the search for God, doubling the effort through each individual's contribution. Such Christ-centered thinking not only enhances our love for our mates, but it emphasizes a godly worldview to our children. It opens the floodgates of communication, service, and selfless love that leaves our spouse speechless and leads our little ones to Christ. Christ's way is simple, stable, and the only surety for success families can find today. May the following devotionals remind you of God's precepts, His perfect plan for families founded in Him. And as you glean truths from His Word, may your love for your mate and your children flourish as you rediscover the beauty of relationships united rightly in Christ.

Bound to Perfection

And He answered and said to them, "Have you not read that He who made them at the beginning 'made them male and female,' and said, 'For this reason a man shall leave his father and mother and be joined to his wife, and the two shall become one flesh'? So then, they are no longer two but one flesh. Therefore what God has joined together, let not man separate."

MATTHEW 19:4–6

God knew he needed more. Adam was king over the ocean, the sky, the trees, the animals—nothing existed that he didn't have, except her. Eve, conceived through Adam's own life, became the necessary angle of a spiritual triangle that helped mankind best see God. With God above and the two below ever seeking His face, inevitably they grew closer together as they neared God's presence, a perfect picture of God's love relationship with His family.

But since the Fall, things haven't been the same. Where love and trust once grew, now seeds of doubt, despair—even divorce—have sprouted like kudzu, covering the accurate picture of hope God intends for His people.

The truth is, Christians are bound to perfection, still. We just don't need to look for it in our mates. Instead, we find our strength and a steady love from above, from our heavenly Father who does not change like shifting shadows. As we receive from Him His endless grace and abounding mercy, we find the freedom to love the spouse God has given us and to allow ourselves the vulnerability required to trust God and our mate. God says that perfect love casts out fear. When we discover God's perfect love for us, our fear of failure, rejection, and of being forgotten simply fades away, and the beauty of Christ's light warms our hearts toward all those around us.

Father,

We have fallen so far from that original picture You painted in Eden for Your children. It is difficult to trust, Lord, because I have felt hurt so many times. I ask You to forgive my doubt, and fill in its place a knowledge and wisdom of Your love for me. Teach me to turn to You and not to others to fill that need for perfect love. And as I receive from You, help me to be the helper, the soul-mate You intend for me to be to my husband.

Heart Reflections
BUILDING FAMILIES OF FAITH

Why do you think divorce is so

rampant today?

What are your own feelings
about it?

What does God have to say
about it?

How can a marriage survive,
even if one spouse is difficult?

Watch Out for Weeds

Pursue peace with all people, and holiness, without which no one will see the Lord: looking carefully lest anyone fall short of the grace of God; lest any root of bitterness springing up cause trouble, and by this many become defiled.

HEBREWS 12:14, 15

There it is again. That nagging sense that something's wrong—a sour attitude that casts a shadow over the rest of the day. It is my warning sign, what I calculate as my joy measurement. When my joy is lacking, I go looking for the root cause—sprouting seeds of bitterness springing up from an ungrateful heart.

At that point I have a choice. I can wallow in the mire of mentally calculated self-pity, or I can confess an unsurrendered heart to the Lord. Confess that I have not been satisfied with His provision in my mate, my circumstances, or my surroundings. Repent and admit that all I really need is Him. When I choose the latter, a miraculous attitude makeover takes place. My husband is off the hook, my children are free to be happy again, and most of all, I sense God's pleasure through His Spirit in me.

So what is your joy measurement these days? Don't wait until it bottoms out and anger bombs explode. Root out wrong thinking now to spare your loved ones and yourself the hurt that bitterness causes. Instead, sow the seeds of contentment and joy.

Father,
Sometimes it is difficult to see seeds of bitterness until they are
full-grown—and almost impossible to weed out. Please help me
to identify any bitterness in my heart, and forgive me for any
ungratefulness toward Your provision for me. I do want to be
at peace with all people, as far as it is possible, and I want
them to see Your holiness in me. Thank You for Your patience,
Lord. Help me to extend it to others.

Heart Reflections

BUILDING FAMILIES OF FAITH

Based on your attitude this week, what is your joy measurement? Why?

Are you aware of any hurts you are harboring in your soul that haunts your relationships?

If you hold bitterness toward your spouse or children, who is affected by it?

Why is it important for us to remove all bitterness and pursue peace and holiness?

Winning Ways

Who can find a virtuous wife? For her worth is far above rubies.
The heart of her husband safely trusts her; so he will have
no lack of gain.

PROVERBS 31:10, 11

It happens in the little things. When he walks through the door at the end of a long day, Thom knows he has my attention. When he's off at his studio, I'm often by his side, helping him sort through priorities of the day, sharing ideas, or simply assembling materials. It is important to me that he knows he comes first in my life—not before God, but because of God. He is the one I vowed to love unconditionally over 18 years ago. He will be the one, God willing, who is holding my hand when my hair turns gray and my strength is gone.

It is not an easy task, particularly with four very needy children clamoring for attention. Mothers have the precarious role of caretaker for so many, while maintaining the priorities God established in His Word. One of the mistakes I've seen so many mothers make is assuming that the children need and deserve our undivided attention, while our husbands don't. Unfortunately, that wrong thinking has left many men feeling unloved and out of the loop.

Trust God that He knows what is best for your family. When He says, "What God has joined together, let no man separate," He is speaking of more than just divorce. Guard your marriage well, and let nothing come between you as husband and wife. In the end your children will rest securely in the love you have for each other, and will hold to the vision of what marriage can and should look like.

Father,

Thank You so much for the precious honor You have given me to love my husband. Help me to be sensitive to his needs, to look for ways to show him that I respect him as the head of our household. I pray that our children will be blessed through our relationship, and that they will grow to experience that same bond of love and commitment in their own future families.

Heart Reflections

BUILDING FAMILIES OF FAITH

*Does your husband rank
highest below God on your
priority list? Why or why not?*

Describe your reception to your husband after work each day.

In what way does your husband need for you to communicate affirmation and respect?

What are some specific ways you can remedy any unbalanced priorities and encourage your husband this week?

Heaven Hears

Again I say to you that if two of you agree on earth concerning anything that they ask, it will be done for them by My Father in heaven. For where two or three are gathered together in My name, I am there in the midst of them.

MATTHEW 18:19, 20

I remember when I held little Winsor in my arms for the first time. She was a miracle from God—so fragile, so tiny—our third little girl, and the answer to over nine months of praying and preparation. But along with her arrival came another gift from the Lord—the opportunity to trust Him. Not long after Winsor had come into this world, the doctors noticed that something was wrong. "Heart murmur," they said. "Potentially life-threatening." "Very critical." These and other horrifying words sank into my ears and heart as I realized that this precious person I held in my arms might not be mine to keep. So Thom and I turned to prayer.

And we prayed hard. Fervently, for weeks, we sought God's face, along with the family of believers at our church. Though I desperately wanted a quick, "Yes, she's healed," "Trust Me" is what I heard instead. We realized that even if we only had a few months with Winsor before the Lord took her home, they were wonderful months that we would not exchange for anything. Though we may never (on this side of heaven) know why He does things the way that He does, we know that He is good, His plans are best, and He sustains our souls.

As it turned out, God chose to spare Winsor. In fact, now she is healthy, happy, and gifted physically and mentally. But each annual trip to the cardiologist is a reminder of God's grace and sovereignty. He does hear our prayers. And He does care. Best of all, He does what He in His wisdom knows is best for His children.

Dear Father,

What a privilege it is to be able to come before You with needs in my life and concern in my heart, knowing that You not only hear my cry, but You are actually present in the midst of my prayers. Father, sometimes Your solution is not what I expect, but by faith in Your Son and in Your Word, I trust my life and my loved ones' lives to You. Thank You for the opportunities You give me to depend on You.

Heart Reflections

BUILDING FAMILIES OF FAITH

Do you really believe prayer works? Why or why not?

Why do you think Jesus said that two must agree on earth in prayer for effectiveness?

With whom can you share your concerns and prayer requests, knowing they will pray with and for you?

How important a role does the body of Christ play in prayer?

Enjoy the Sunset

*Therefore, putting away lying, "Let each one of you speak truth
with his neighbor," for we are members of one another. "Be angry,
and do not sin": do not let the sun go down on your wrath,
nor give place to the devil.*

EPHESIANS 4:25–27

We have been best friends since the age of twelve. Now
after more than 18 years of marriage, Thom and I are still
talking—lots. The trick to our untiring devotion to each
other? Simply put, it is God. God in the details of our
every day, evidencing Himself through our actions, our
words, even our thoughts.

That's why it is impossible for us to let the sun go down
on unresolved issues. Since we don't have television or
computers in our home that could possibly be used as
distractions, we are faced with each other. We can't
escape it—we have to talk it out. The Holy Spirit in our
hearts urges us to it, and our commitment to our
marriage and to Him seals the deal.

It's not that there is always immediate resolution. Thom and I are both strong and opinionated people. But when there is dissension among the ranks, we wait before the Lord until He makes Himself clear to both parties. Biblically, Thom is the commanding officer, so to speak, of our little brigade. But he does not make decisions apart from the full support of the troops. It is a safeguard for both of us to wait patiently on God's timing and direction. When our eyes are on Him, our selfish agendas surrender to God's sovereign will. Suddenly, peace shines like a beautiful sunset over our souls, and we're able to enjoy the view together.

Father,
Satan would love to undermine my family, my marriage, and
my relationship with You through my own self-centeredness.
Help me to put to death the desires of the flesh and to consider
others as more important than myself. Help me, too, to stay
focused on You, my Leader, that I would walk where You
lead—in Your time. Thank You for my husband. Help him to
see You in all he does and empower him to lead our family
closer to You.

Heart Reflections

BUILDING FAMILIES OF FAITH

How is it possible to be angry

and not sin?

How does anger serve as a warning siren for something else lurking in your heart?

Why do you think God prefaces the verse about anger with a statement about telling the truth?

How can we be the initiators of peace in our family?

Light the Candelabra

Do all things without complaining and disputing, that you may become blameless and harmless, children of God without fault in the midst of a crooked and perverse generation, among whom you shine as lights in the world.

PHILIPPIANS 2:14, 15

The little boy sitting next to Merritt in her first-grade class had no clue what was coming. "Do you believe in Jesus?" she inquired, as soft and steady as a spring rain. Somewhat shocked by the question, the Jewish boy stammered, "Well, sort of. I think He was a good prophet. I'm half-Jew, half-Christian."

Then came the downpour. In less than a minute, Merritt quickly corrected his theology and matter-of-factly let him know that hell was waiting if he didn't trust in Jesus. It was a sudden shower of truth, rawly spoken out of the tender eagerness of one so young, but it represented the passion for Christ and for truth that Thom and I have prayed for and worked to instill in each of our girls. (We're still working on the presentation!)

Our ministry is clear to our family—and it is not limited to Thom's paintings alone. Each of us shares a unique perspective of God and His grace with the rest of those around us. Regardless of age, our actions and inner character communicate to others what God's gospel of love and peace through Christ is all about. It is almost as if individually we are lights in the world—like the lights in Thom's paintings. But when those lights are held closely together, they burn with a brighter intensity than ever before, clearly shining the way to the Savior.

Father,

You have called our family to stand apart from the ways of the world, and to shine Christ's light in the midst of darkness. But without Your Spirit in our lives, our light is snuffed out. Come, Lord, and fill Your people. Open the doors of opportunity to love and lead others to You. Empower me with childlike boldness, and remove from my heart a critical and complaining spirit, that Your light may shine unhindered.

Heart Reflections

BUILDING FAMILIES OF FAITH

In your family, do you feel alone spiritually or are you a part of a spiritual team? Why?

Why do you think God singles
out complaining and disputing
as the two vices we must
eliminate in order to shine
blameless and harmless in His
universe?

How can you encourage your
spouse and your children to
shine Christ's light in the
world?

Is there anyone with whom you
and your family need to share
the gospel of Christ? If so, how
do you plan to do it?

Learning to Love

And now abide faith, hope, love, these three;
but the greatest of these is love.
1 CORINTHIANS 13:13

I love to cook. It is one of my secret joys—a simple way that I can give to another individual an edible version of my love and concern.

As a family, we also support several young Guatemalan children whose circumstances demand that help be received from outside the home. We have prayed for each of them, written them letters, and have even gone to visit two of them, sharing with them necessities for life we had brought with us from the States.

But what I have come to learn about true love is this: Non-Christians can cook (as well or better than I). Even without Christ, people can still contribute to a host of charities that really do help the world from a physical standpoint. So what is the difference between what non-Christians can do and the kind of love to which God calls His children?

It is demonstrated through Jesus Christ, the Author of true love. In essence, it is the absence of self. No judging. No self-righteousness. No searching for wrong motives. Only a proactive extension of the grace that flows to us from our Father's heart. It is the kind of love that takes us beyond simply writing a check or cooking a casserole to entering into another's place of pain with them and embracing them just as they are. Even as Christ comforted the tax collector, protected the prostitute, and healed the hurts of the world's most homely, we, too, reveal our Creator's compassion when we leave comfort zones behind and engage the world around us with real relationships that reconnect them with hope.

Father,

When I see how You define love, it becomes painfully obvious that apart from You I am incapable of the kind of love You want from me. But I praise You because You can actually love others through me. Not only do You heal physical hurts, but You also reach into the deepest recesses of our hearts and resurrect new spiritual life. Jesus, I need You to empty me of myself so Your Spirit can fill me and lead me to a life of love for others like You demonstrated for me.

Heart Reflections

BUILDING FAMILIES OF FAITH

What's the easiest way for you to demonstrate your love toward someone?

What is the most sacrificial
way you have ever
demonstrated your love?

What is the most encouraging
or challenging part of
1 Corinthians 13?

Name some ways you feel God
is calling you to love others
with His love.

Walk and Work

For we are His workmanship, created in Christ Jesus for good works, which God prepared beforehand that we should walk in them.

EPHESIANS 2:10

Did you know that God has ordained every single work He has prepared for you to do? What a privilege, then, we have as Christians to single-mindedly focus on the tasks that Christ Himself sets before us. The question for us is: What exactly are those works, and how will I know what to do?

Again, God's beautiful plan comes into play. He sums it up in one of my favorite verses that I keep posted by my sink at home. Proverbs 3:5, 6 says, "Trust in the LORD with all your heart, and lean not on your own understanding; in all your ways acknowledge Him, and He shall direct your paths." As the Good Shepherd, God knows where He is leading us. Though we may walk over rocky places, down in the valley, or up on top of mountain peaks, He is faithful to lead us home, forming the character of Christ in us all the while. And as we commit all the tiny details of our day over to Him and ask for His guidance, He swings wide the doors we were born to walk through—to not only witness His glory, but also to actively participate in the building of His kingdom. It's incredibly freeing to realize that we don't have to do everything. We just walk in the works God has ordained for us. He'll take care of us and the rest, too.

Father,

Thank You that Your plan for my life existed even before this world did. Thank You that even in my faithless times, You are faithful to guide me to Your truth. Direct my feet, Lord, that I might walk in all the works You have prepared for me, and help me to not be distracted by any other thing which You have reserved for other members of Your body to do.

Heart Reflections

BUILDING FAMILIES OF FAITH

Have you ever volunteered for service without consulting the Lord first? What was the result?

Have you ever obeyed God's call to action where you saw Him at work? What was the result?

Describe what it means to you to "acknowledge" God.

If you feel overwhelmed by responsibilities, list them here. Pray over each one and ask the Lord to show you what is and is not from Him.

Proper Parenting

"Honor your father and mother," which is the first commandment with promise: "that it may be well with you and you may live long on the earth."

EPHESIANS 6:2, 3

His father left them when Thom was only five. Three children and one lonely woman now faced life without a dad, without a husband. Life was difficult to say the least, but it was not without love. Thom's mom worked hard not only to make ends meet, but also to mend hurting hearts.

Of course, as an adult the tables have turned for Thom. God has blessed his work, and he provides well for his family. Committed not only to the girls and me, Thom relentlessly seeks ways to relieve any stress from his mom's life, and literally searches out creative ways to make her smile.

But what about his father?

First, Thom found him, still stuck in the same hole of

apathy and alienation he had fallen into so many years ago. To get him out, Thom gave him a paintbrush, a palette, and persuaded him to simply try. Thom even bought his dad's finished work. But it was his father who really got the picture, the one that said, "I still love you. And I forgive you." It was a forgiveness he desperately needed from his son, and also from his heavenly Father. He found it from both, and in his late seventies, he surrendered his life to the Lord.

In very different ways, both parents are still alive today as a testament of God's grace, and the rich rewards we experience when we honor them.

Father,

Thank You for giving me my parents. Though they are not perfect, they are Your perfect choice for me, and I am grateful for them. Please show me ways in which I can continue to honor them, even into their old age. And help me to instill the same values in our children, that it may go well with them, too.

Heart Reflections

BUILDING FAMILIES OF FAITH

What does God mean when
He says to "honor" our parents?

Why do you think this is the
first of God's commandments
with a promise?

What are some ways you can
begin or continue to honor
your parents?

How can you begin to
encourage this act of obedience
in your own children?

Laughing Out Love

*A merry heart does good, like medicine, but a broken
spirit dries the bones.*

PROVERBS 17:22

It never fails. Tensions have been high all day. We've hurried here. Been there. Done too much. And dangling on the edge of coming undone ourselves when . . . in he walks. Unaware of our harried day, he has no idea of what is coming. Suddenly, like a neon light attracting a host of moths, Thom is attacked by our girls—all flying from different directions declaring their intentions, "Let's hop on Pop!"

Suddenly all the stress of the day melts away into a million tickles and giggles as Thom wallows under a pile of writhing, wriggling, now-happy little girls. Of course, the laughter is contagious. And I marvel at the miracle of simply lightening up and smiling out the stress.

In fact, tickles, jokes, and giggles have become our family's favorite way of showing affection. It is a very tangible way to keep in touch with one another. Laughter is one of God's most precious gifts, one that we as Christians unfortunately overlook all too often. So the next time you feel life's pressures piling up on you, take them to God. Talk them out with your mate. But don't take it too seriously. Smile instead, and surround others with the knowledge of your love and God's!

Father,

Sometimes I get so serious about life it's hard to think that You smile—even laugh. Jesus, I rejoice that You are in control of all things, and I know that anxiety and stress are simply signs that I am not fully trusting You. Forgive me, Lord, and replace the stress with the silly, happy, giddy joy I can get from knowing You. May it be contagious to others, too.

Heart Reflections

BUILDING FAMILIES OF FAITH

*How can having a happy heart
change the way we perceive
life's events?*

How would you describe the general tone or atmosphere in your home?

What would you like for it to be?

What are some ways you can help cultivate a fun- and love-filled home?

Making Moments

See then that you walk circumspectly, not as fools but as wise,
redeeming the time, because the days are evil.

EPHESIANS 5:15, 16

Home is a wonderful place. It's where I feel free to make a fool of myself, and the girls only love me all the more for it. For us, home is our license for unadulterated, unashamed fun—from the most menial tasks to the most special treats that come our way. Cooking dinner doesn't just mean making a meal. It means working as a team to test the speed limits on how fast Merritt can peel a carrot, or how quickly Chandler can set the table. Instead of a chore, it's a challenge. And instead of just another mundane event, for our girls it becomes a moment to remember.

All of life is made up of potentially memorable moments . . . if we take the time to make them worth remembering. After all, we are only on earth for a very short time. So why not make the very most of what God gives us?

Whether it's reading stories with all the melodrama you dare to muster, or singing every silly song in the book as you travel from one place to another, by all means, celebrate life. It's found in the details, in the day-to-day. And it's the difference that can not only change your tune, but also give your loved ones a new song to sing for the rest of their lives.

Father,

Thank You for life. In every detail of every day, there is joy to be found in You. Help me to see it, Lord, and share it with those who are around me. And in the sad times, God, I will remember those precious moments, and sing Your joyful songs of praise to set my soul free once more.

Heart Reflections

BUILDING FAMILIES OF FAITH

What is your most favorite

family moment?

What makes these moments special to you?

_____

_____

_____

_____

_____

How can you make each moment count on a daily basis?

_____

_____

_____

_____

Name some specific things you want to do today to change an ordinary event into something extraordinary.

_____

_____

_____

_____

Along the Way

And these words which I command you today shall be in your heart. You shall teach them diligently to your children, and shall talk of them when you sit in your house, when you walk by the way, when you lie down, and when you rise up.

DEUTERONOMY 6:6, 7

Our girls get their formal teaching from many different places—Sunday school, youth group and church activities, and school, to name a few. But the bedrock of belief, the real shape of their worldview, is built by the prayers we pray throughout the day.

Like when we come upon an overflowing parking lot and need a space. We simply ask God to reserve us one. Or whenever someone gets hurt, we ask Jesus for healing. Even if we hear a siren, we'll stop what we're doing and lift that unknown soul up to Him. And when He answers, we pray again—this time to give thanks. Thanks that He is a God of details, and He cares and controls even the tiniest details of our day.

For all of us, the habit of prayer has formed a foundational focus on Christ in all circumstances. Talking to God is not just an exercise performed before meals or bedtime. Instead, it is the very essence of living, of walking moment by moment with God at our side. He is included throughout the day. And we are entirely dependent on His blessed presence.

So as you seek to raise your little ones in the Lord, remember to teach them truth and to memorize it. But most important is to live it, and that only happens through lives surrendered to the Lord in prayer.

Father,
It is incredible to think that the God of the universe is
intimately acquainted with all my ways. What a blessing to not
only come to You with every thought, hurt, need, or praise, but
to take my children with me before Your throne. Empower me
through Your Spirit to pray without ceasing, and give me the
wisdom I need to raise my children according to Your Word.

Heart Reflections

BUILDING FAMILIES OF FAITH

How much of a role does prayer play in your life personally, as well as in your family's?

What keeps you from praying
more often?

Name some ways you can lead
your family into prayer
throughout the day.

Record here any special prayer
requests for this week and the
answer God gives.

Love in Action

We've worshipped the Father. Worked with our families. And now it's time to face the world, renewed with a spirit of hope and strength. Nourished from our time with Christ, our lives are ready to bear the fruit of His presence in us, the evidence of His Spirit conforming us to His image. Attitudes of worship transform into works of obedience, the language of hearts so touched by His love that they must speak in action.

And there's a lot of work to be done. Homes to mend. Needy to feed and clothe. Prisons to visit. Relationships to reconcile. Nursing homes to entertain. The lonely to encourage. The list goes on, and we know in our hearts just how sorely we're needed. It is here in the call to action where we actually have the opportunity to lay down our lives as Christ did for us. We take up His cross of service and self-sacrifice, and watch the wonders of God as He uses emptied lives for the filling of His glory.

The following devotionals provide a framework for service in Christ's kingdom. They are certainly not exhaustive, but the scriptural principles outlined help establish a basic understanding of how we discern God's will for our lives as we live in a world so desperately in need of Christ's love. The emphasis is on emptying us of ourselves and filling our hearts and minds with Christ, instead. They draw attention to the obvious needs, exhort us to action, and encourage us to persevere in our high and precious calling. May God bless you as you read these truths and enable you to remember them when you are down in the trenches. In the end, may the body of Christ hear the blessed words, "Well done, My good and faithful servant."

Remember Him

Abide in Me, and I in you. As the branch cannot bear fruit of itself, unless it abides in the vine, neither can you, unless you abide in Me.

JOHN 15:4

At first it might seem a little odd to consecrate creativity to the Lord. But from the very beginning of our business with Thom's work, we believed that every article that came from Thom's hand should be prayed over and given over to the Lord. Thom's artistic ability to capture scenes of peace and serenity did not originate from him, though to the world they may seem novel ideas. In reality, each piece is inspired by the light and love Thom has come to know from the Lord. It overflows onto the canvas and creates beautiful pictures of a hope that, without Christ, we could never have.

God paints the same lesson in every area of life for us. Though we may think we have control over our success—that if we work hard enough we can secure our faith and our future—the fact is, "the branch cannot bear fruit of itself." Or as Psalm 127:1 puts it, "Unless the LORD builds the house, they labor in vain who build it." To produce works of any eternal significance is entirely dependent on an eternal God empowering our efforts. Apart from Him, we can do nothing.

The implications are enormous in the way we approach our work. We strive, but only in His strength. We prepare, but only after committing it to prayer. And we act, but we move forward in the knowledge that He directs our paths, and He alone can produce the fruit.

Father,

How humbling it is to realize that even my best efforts are worthless if they do not originate from You. Forgive me for the arrogance that has made me ever think otherwise. I surrender myself to You, and ask that You will fill me, lead me, and produce in me the beautiful work of righteousness that truly touches the heart of eternity.

Heart Reflections

BUILDING FAMILIES OF FAITH

What does it mean to abide in

Christ?

How can we know whether or
not our works originate from
Christ or ourselves?

Living in pride or insecurity
helps us to know that we are
not abiding in Christ. Are there
any areas of your life where
these attitudes dominate?

Enter into His rest. Record here
the areas in your life you must
surrender again to abide in
Christ.

Take Heart

And let us not grow weary while doing good, for in due season we shall reap if we do not lose heart. Therefore, as we have opportunity, let us do good to all, especially to those who are of the household of faith.

GALATIANS 6:9, 10

It is a new day, and as the foggy vision of sleepiness clears, the mountain of clothes to be laundered looms into view. Then come the thoughts of floors that need mopping, furniture that needs dusting, and that pie you promised to bake. Not to mention, of course, the whole routine required to get the kids off to school. It seems that before your feet ever touch the floor, you're tired again.

Sometimes it's the menial tasks of everyday life that can take the most out of women. Perhaps because of its repetitive nature. Or maybe because our efforts are not always noticed. Not even paid. It is here that Satan hopes to defeat us—to distract us from the proper perspective, which (as in all things) is still found in Christ.

For Jesus Christ knows what it is to serve an inattentive and ungrateful world. The King of all creation actually washed His disciples' feet. He died for people who didn't even like Him. What an honor, then, it is for us women to be able to serve others in the same capacity as Christ. Whether it's wiping little noses or cleaning off countertops, the more things we have to do, the more opportunities we have to bring Him honor. Though no one else may see or care, God does. And He receives each effort as a gift of thanks for the incredible sacrifice He gave us—Christ Himself.

Father,
What a wonderful calling You have given women to be able to
serve in so many ways. Free me, Lord, from the sin of
comparison and complaining, and instead fill me with a
grateful heart that sees the best in every circumstance. Help me
to remember that in everything I do—even in the smallest
things—I do them for Your glory. Help me, too, to hold
steady, knowing that the efforts produced by Your Spirit in me
are never in vain.

Heart Reflections

BUILDING FAMILIES OF FAITH

What is the purpose of

Galatians 6:9, 10?

Why is it important to encourage one another to love and good works?

What does God promise to do if we persevere?

What are some specific ways you can minister to the body of Christ and others around you?

All or Nothing

Therefore, whether you eat or drink, or whatever you do,
do all to the glory of God.

1 CORINTHIANS 10:31

At first glance at our public lives, people may marvel at our ministry's magnitude. "It must be incredible to be used by God like that—to reach people all around the world through beautiful paintings," they'll often say. All of us stand amazed at the few Billy Grahams and Mother Theresas of the world—those select few who through speaking, writing, or service seem to stand in a special place with God to win the world to Christ. And we'll think, "That's great that God uses them like that," never dreaming that each of His children have the same calling.

It's not that we all have to accomplish some great work of art, preach from a podium to millions, or live among the world's most destitute. Your audience may be as few as the number in your family who learn from you the foundations of faith. Maybe it's a classroom full of kids who would only see or hear about God from you. Or simply the people in your workplace. No matter what we do or what our lives look like, we must do it all and only for God's glory. Paul says that even in what we eat and drink, our actions should direct honor to Him. Having magnificent ministries is not, then, dependent upon the size of the crowd, but upon the complete focus on God's glory through life's every detail. Maybe you will have the privilege of seeing the impact your life lived in Christ has had on those around you. Or maybe God will reserve that prize when you take your place in heaven. Whichever, we must realize that God wants all of us, all the time. In that total surrender of ourselves we offer up a pleasing sacrifice to Him—a sacrifice that He can and will use to further His kingdom and bring Himself glory in the most miraculous ways.

Father,

I admit that I often think You leave it up to others to have worldwide impact for Your kingdom. I often forget that through prayer and faithful living Your Spirit is released to touch people's hearts all across the globe. Help me to obey Your calling for me—to surrender every area of my life to You as a sacrifice of obedience and praise. And use me however You want to do it. I gladly leave the results to You.

Heart Reflections

BUILDING FAMILIES OF FAITH

What does it mean to "do all to the glory of God"?

Is there any area of your life
exempt from this command?

....

....

....

....

....

What is the result of a
completely surrendered life in
God's hands?

....

....

....

....

....

Can you think of a time when
God used you for the building
of His kingdom?

....

....

....

You First

But Jesus called them to Himself and said, "You know that the rulers of the Gentiles lord it over them, and those who are great exercise authority over them. Yet it shall not be so among you; but whoever desires to become great among you, let him be your servant."

MATTHEW 20:25, 26

It's one thing to say it at an intersection, a doorway, or a grocery line. It's another to put others first in every area, at every moment—even in your heart and mind. But it is the service to which Christ calls us.

The opposite of selflessness, namely selfishness, stems from two basic roots. The first is the sin of pride, which puffs up our own importance in our minds, causing us to think that intrinsically we are better than the people around us. The other is actually fear—fear that if we put other people first our needs will be forgotten, and we will become the proverbial doormat over which the rest of the world will gladly walk.

But when we're rooted in Christ, there is no room for such weeds. He tells us that all of us are sinners, justly deserving His displeasure. Only in Him do we have any value at all—so much for pride! The good news, though, is that He loves us perfectly, which casts out our fears of neglect and abandonment. Suddenly, we are freed to see the beauty that Christ sees in other people—His wonderful creation. He fills us with the same servant spirit He demonstrated for us when He set aside His royal status to serve sinners. Knowing that He meets our needs above and beyond our expectations enables us to serve others with reckless abandon and rest in the love He extends to us.

Father,
I confess as sin my prideful thoughts that put me before others.
I know that in You I am a coheir with Christ, an adopted
child of God, and I am wholly and dearly loved. But apart
from You I am nothing. In humility, I ask You to help me see
others through Your eyes of grace, and to lavish on them the
same unconditional love You have shown me.

Heart Reflections
BUILDING FAMILIES OF FAITH

Why do you think it is so
difficult to put others first?

Why does Christ insist that we do so?

What role did humility play in Christ's life?

What role should it play in yours?

Growing Up

But also for this very reason, giving all diligence, add to your faith
virtue, to virtue knowledge, to knowledge self-control, to self-control
perseverance, to perseverance godliness, to godliness brotherly
kindness, and to brotherly kindness love. For if these things are
yours and abound, you will be neither barren nor unfruitful in the
knowledge of our Lord Jesus Christ.

2 PETER 1:5–8

When Christ offered abundant life, He meant much
more than simply knowing about salvation. The moment
we become new creatures, we embark on an incredible
journey of an ever-deepening faith and knowledge of
God.

I think my relationship with Him started with the basic
recognition of my deep need for God. It wasn't difficult
for me to see that I was a sinner who needed a Savior.
But it grew from there to real dependence upon God. I
could no longer approach life's trials under my own
power because my knowledge of His sovereignty had
grown too strong. As I realized His position of power in
my life, and that God indeed is good, a tremendous trust

formed and framed a beautiful friendship that I now share with the Creator of my soul. It is a wonderful walk with Him, where day by day He opens my eyes to see new, exciting, and awe-inspiring elements of His character.

The relationship comes moment by moment as I stand firm on the scriptural foundation He has already formed in my life. Looking forward, He leads me deeper into His heart. And as I find more of Him and share it with others, my journey forges a way for others to follow. It is a blessed calling He has given us—the exquisite process of knowing Him, becoming holy, and helping others find Him, too.

Father,

What a wonderful plan You have prepared for me! You delight in my search for You, and You have promised to reveal Yourself to me. Help me to remember life's lessons You have taught me along the way, that I might build upon those foundational truths to get a better glimpse of Your glory. Change me, mold me, and make me the person You want me to be. It is a lifelong process, and I rejoice in Your lifelong friendship.

Heart Reflections

BUILDING FAMILIES OF FAITH

Restate the process of spiritual

growth found in 2 Peter 1:5–8

in your own words.

*If we see this pattern of growth
in our lives, what does God
promise?*

*How has your understanding
of God changed since you first
became a Christian?*

*Briefly record your spiritual
journey here, as well as your
prayer for the future.*

Simply Put

He has shown you, O man, what is good; and what does the LORD require of you but to do justly, to love mercy, and to walk humbly with your God?

MICAH 6:8

Have you ever stopped and wondered what God's will is for your life? It seems to be a deep question. Almost rhetorical. Ripe for discussion. And somewhere down the road you might just discover it. Knowing God's will for our lives often seems more mysterious than mandatory, more elusive than something God intends for us to experience.

But when we lose sight of the work God is building in us, we have to refer back to God's blueprint—His Word. Granted, His outline is not as defined as we may want. Micah 6:8 sums up our calling as Christians as simply to do justly, to love mercy, and to walk humbly with God. That's it. No earthshaking, mind-blowing revelation to tell you exactly what to do. Instead, He tells us how to be.

I think He does that for two reasons. One, if He clearly told us what specific thing to do, we'd be off and running in that direction without waiting on His timing. The other is that God is as concerned with attitude as with action. He's not up in heaven hoping we get together the right to-do list; He wants right hearts. That happens when we acknowledge Him in all our ways, trusting that He alone will direct our paths at the right time. By living simply in Him, surrendered to Him, discerning God's will is no longer stressful. Instead, it becomes first nature as every moment of our lives is directed by His Spirit.

Father,
Thank You that You do have a "will" for my life. I'm
beginning to see that instead of it necessarily being something
You have for me to accomplish, it is someone You want me to
become. Help empty me of myself that Your Spirit may come
and fill me. Then, day by day, as I encounter new
opportunities, decisions, and challenges, I can rest in Your
guidance as I simply seek to do justly, to love mercy, and to
walk humbly with You.

Heart Reflections

BUILDING FAMILIES OF FAITH

What does it mean to "do justly"?

What does it mean to "love mercy"?

What does it mean to "walk humbly with God"?

How will doing these three things in Christ's strength revolutionize your life?

In Lieu of the Lost

Pure and undefiled religion before God and the Father is this: to visit orphans and widows in their trouble, and to keep oneself unspotted from the world.

JAMES 1:27

You know the scenario. You're innocently walking into your church, ready to sit down and listen for God's message to you, when along the way your eye catches a new, little booth on the side of the foyer. Since you have arrived early, you go over and pick up a brochure picturing a dark-skinned child from a country halfway around the world. His belly is distended, and a pitiful plea for help stares up at you through hurting eyes. The reaction? For some, they just feel sad for the poor people, and hope to soon put the image out of their minds. There are too many hurting people for one person to help. "Once I break down and give to one, what about the millions of others?" they may ask. It's easier to ignore and hope someone else—someone with more money—heeds the call.

But God is the hero of the homeless. He's the champion for children who have no food, no running water, even no parents. He's the husband for widows. And He calls on His own family to feed them. Clothe them. Love them, and lead them to Him. If His body would simply obey, the task at hand would not seem so overwhelming. But we often neglect our duty—our honor and high calling—by our own self-centered lifestyles.

If we are to walk in obedience, to really live out God's love, we must look to Him for His direction. Where does He want us to spend our time? Our money? As we realize that every moment we have and every penny we own truly belongs to Him, it is easier to relinquish our hold and surrender to the gentle guidance of His Holy Spirit. Then we realize the truth Christ wanted to teach us when He said, "It is more blessed to give than to receive" (Acts 20:35).

Father,
There are a lot of gray areas in Scripture open to interpretation, but the instruction to take care of orphans and widows is not one of them. The task is large and, apart from You, impossible. Please open my eyes to see exactly where You want me to participate—whether it is in my own church, community, or a country around the world. I am open to Your leading. All that I have is Yours. I look forward to participating with You in Your work of restoration and healing.

Heart Reflections

BUILDING FAMILIES OF FAITH

What, if anything, hinders you

from reaching out to others?

Are you aware of any needs in your church?

What are some ways you can minister to the people God has placed in your path?

How can you help involve your husband and children in the ministry?

Spoken Strength

And let us consider one another in order to stir up love and good works, not forsaking the assembling of ourselves together, as is the manner of some, but exhorting one another, and so much the more as you see the Day approaching.

HEBREWS 10:24, 25

It was a simple step of faith. A friend of mine suggested we set aside a time of prayer each week so that together we could lift up our husbands and our newly started businesses to the Lord. But as we met, something simple became supernatural. As sisters in Christ we bonded together in ways we never knew possible. Through trials and praises we persevered together in prayer and witnessed the beautiful work of "iron sharpening iron" in each other's lives.

Today our meeting of two has turned into a larger group of women who meet to pray, encourage, and hold each other accountable. And I speak for the whole lot of us— it's a pivotal point of empowerment, encouragement, and support that we receive from each other and God each week.

Let's face it. In life today the commodity of connection can hardly be found. Christians seem scattered with over-stuffed schedules. But for a time we can put them aside. Pick up the phone and call on your women friends who you know really care about the Lord. Get together—as friends, as members of the body of Christ—and come before the Lord. There's a never-ending fountain of refreshment for you there.

Father,
It sounds so inviting—the idea of fellowship with women that
builds us up in our faith. But when it all comes down, the
other demands of the day seem more realistic. I know that in
my heart I doubt that Your call to stay connected is as
important as all my other goals. I confess it as sin and ask You
to show me the women with whom I need to initiate
relationships. Help us set aside a time where we, together, can
turn to You for help and strength.

Heart Reflections

BUILDING FAMILIES OF FAITH

Describe your relationship to the

body of Christ—particularly

with the women in your church.

Do you have a core group of
friends to hold you accountable
to God's Word? Why or why
not?

Can you think of some women
God has put on your heart to
call?

Name some specific ways you
plan to initiate relationships
with them this week.

Ties That Bind

It is convenient that Thom works right beside our home, not simply because of the short commute, but more for his instant accessibility. When exciting, discouraging, or shocking news happens, I can walk right out the door and into his studio where I inevitably find an avid listener waiting to hear the latest. It is a profound friendship that I have in my husband—a bond that staves off loneliness, encourages steadiness, and secures support that keeps me sailing through life. It also serves as a reminder to me of the same kind of relationship the Lord longs to have with me, too, as a constant companion for the rest of my life.

Many times when we think of friends, our thoughts turn immediately to those we love around us. It is natural and biblical to do so. Scripture says that "two are better than one, because they have a good reward for their labor. For if they fall, one will lift up his companion." It goes on to say, "Again, if two lie down together, they will keep warm; but how can one be warm alone?" (Eccl. 4:9–11). From the beginning of time until now God has given us the blessings of family and friendships that form life's very fabric. Throughout Scripture God exhorts us to die to ourselves that we might look after the needs of others—in essence to be the very friends that each of us want and need so badly.

But as important as our horizontal relationships with others may be, our vertical relationship with God stands as the foundational friendship before and for all others. As our relationship with God is reconciled, we forsake the world and its ways that distract our heavenly focus. Much like Thom's studio is for me, prayer is the Christian's immediate access to a caring and concerned audience—God the Father, Son, and Holy Spirit. No matter what the news, God knows and understands it and is ready to impart the wisdom and grace we need to handle it. And unlike any of our earthly friendships, we can always count on His unconditional love, forgiveness, and availability from now until eternity.

As you read the following devotionals, may your heart be encouraged toward your brothers and sisters in Christ. May your faith be strengthened to resist the world's fickle friendship. And may your focus be renewed on the Friend who sticks by you closer than a brother. Only heaven offers the most profound friendship on earth—the instant, accessible, and eternal friendship with God.

Still There

A man who has friends must himself be friendly, but there is a friend who sticks closer than a brother.

PROVERBS 18:24

Like colors on a palette, loneliness comes in many shades. In my life I've only experienced the lighter hues because Thom and the children surround me with so much love and companionship. Our tightly knit clan has weathered together so many storms of life that, regardless of where the tide of public opinion may rise or fall, we feel confident that we can forge ahead because we have God and each other at our side.

The scariest times of my life have been those awkward, silent moments where the One who keeps our family so close seems to be hiding. Suddenly, the shade of loneliness deepens as the core substance of my soul seems so far away. I'll pray, but hear no voice. I'll ask for direction, and receive only silence. It is at these precarious moments that I realize that, even as much as

I love my family, and need and want their fellowship, without the Lord life itself is for naught.

The good news is God never leaves us stranded. Though He may remain quiet for His own reasons, at His right time He opens the floodgates of communication and speaks peace to our hearts, "Fear not, for I am with you." The knowledge that the God of creation and Savior of the world is always by my side colors my outlook with such brilliant hope that it transforms the palor of loneliness into a prism of God's glorious light.

Father,

It is so easy for me to look to the people around me for the comfort and companionship I so desperately crave. While I know that it was part of Your design for us to draw strength from each other, I need to remember that You are my best Friend, the One who knows my deepest, darkest secrets—and yet You still love me and want to be with me. Thank You for Your faithfulness to stay by my side through all of life's stages. Please keep me close to Your heart.

Heart Reflections

BUILDING FAMILIES OF FAITH

Why do we continue to seek comfort from everyone else but Christ?

Why do you think God allows loneliness in our lives?

In what ways is Christ our best friend?

How can we foster that relationship?

The Wrong Crowd

Adulterers and adulteresses! Do you not know that friendship with the world is enmity with God? Whoever therefore wants to be a friend of the world makes himself an enemy of God.

JAMES 4:4

I've heard the horror stories—the ones about how sweet, little children turn into big, defiant teens who tamper with every temptation that comes their way. And from the evidence I see around me, I know the rumors may hold some truth. The warnings actually help spur on our prayers and daily practices of obeying biblical directives so that later, when the moments of decision come for our kids, God's Word will be so ingrained in them that they can easily see right from wrong and will choose to walk in the right path.

But as I'm coaching my kids, I realize that even seasoned Christians face a similar threat—maybe even more insidious than the first. The lure of the world—what the Bible calls the lust of the flesh, the lust of the eyes, and the boastful pride of life—is intensely strong. Not only is it "out there" where actual material possessions lie, but it also attacks from within our own hearts. While our renewed spirit may want to focus on things above, if left unchecked our flesh will latch hold of whatever it can to distract us from Christ and His kingdom.

Scripture says the fruit of the flesh is evident. Whenever depression, anger, or other bad habits begin to manifest themselves in my life, I am aware that my attention has shifted from my first love to a worldly lust. As it does for our children, God's Word bears testimony to the truth and lights my way back to a better worldview—the one where Christ reigns in control and the world's grip is lost in His grace.

Father,

I am amazed to realize that I never outgrow the temptation to be led by the wrong crowd. Left on my own, I leave what is good and cling to what doesn't last. Forgive me, and renew my mind through Your Word. Help me to let go of the things of this world—the desire for wealth, prestige, power, popularity—and to cling solely to You. Help me to heed Your warnings and to walk with You all the days of my life.

Heart Reflections
BUILDING FAMILIES OF FAITH

*What does it mean to be a
friend of the world?*

*Why can't we be at peace with
God and the world at the same
time?*

What does God say He does to
those who are lukewarm?

Are there any warning signs
in your life that indicate a
growing affection for the
world? What are they?

What can you do to reverse the
process?

Love Language

Greater love has no one than this, than to lay down one's life for his friends.

JOHN 15:13

As Americans we love lots of things. Of course, we love our families, our friends, and our faith. But we also love pizza, football, and Fridays. In a land of such plenty, the word *love* has come to encompass so much that the definition itself has become trivialized and its spoken meaning almost hollow.

But there is a love language replete with power that has transcended the ages. In word it's defined in 1 Corinthians 13. But in action we find it in Christ. God didn't just tell us He loved us; He proved it, again and again. Just imagine for a moment—a holy God providing a plan for His people's salvation. Removing royal robes and relinquishing glory to humbly serve the creatures He created. And serve He did. Relentlessly, despite rejection and ridicule, He offered up Himself for the betterment of those who didn't deserve it at all. Through His prayers and His teachings, Jesus did speak words of love to many. But when the words were silent, His life shouted the message louder than ever.

As His followers we are called to no less than our Leader. For Christians, fairness is not the issue. Even sharing isn't the main point. The greatest joy comes from giving—of laying down our lives moment by moment, issue by issue, that Christ might fill us with Himself.

Father,
When I consider all the ramifications of Your ultimate
sacrifice—Your own Son—I stand amazed. Forgive me for
putting my priorities first before Yours and others, and thus for
having wrong priorities. Teach me what You mean when You
tell me to die to myself, to lay down my life for others. It
sounds scary, but by faith I trust in You, knowing that in
losing my life I will truly find it in You.

Heart Reflections

BUILDING FAMILIES OF FAITH

What examples can you think of that demonstrate society's definition of love?

Why does a Christian's
definition of love differ from
the world's?

What is the best way we can
show Christ our love and
devotion?

What does it mean to lay down
our life for Christ? For others?

Victory in Vulnerability

Confess your trespasses to one another, and pray for one another, that you may be healed. The effective, fervent prayer of a righteous man avails much.

JAMES 5:16

We have all encountered well-meaning Christians—the ones who, just when you think you've hit your lowest point, come in to criticize your commitment or chastise you because of your crisis—who have the idea that their words will help you get your act together. Instead, they leave us wondering what happened to all the love that God's Word says should define the body of Christ.

Yet James exhorts us to trust this faulty body of followers. To confess our sins to one another and pray with each other for encouragement. Was he out of his mind? Had he never been burnt by a brother? Chances are, he had, for sin is nothing new to God's children. But James was pointing to the picture of holiness and unity Christ intends for His people. It is a portrait that cannot happen simply individually. It unfolds collectively as His children conform to His plan of worshipping Him with one heart and mind.

As in all areas of our lives, we must listen to the Spirit's direction. Through His wisdom, we choose our closest friends with whom we can confide: friends who listen before they speak, and when they do speak, their conversation is seasoned with God's gracious love; fellow sisters in Christ who earnestly seek His face and His kingdom, whom you can count on to stand with you in the trenches of prayer until all of life's trials are past. These kinds of people are few, but they can be found if you seek them out—and if you become one of them yourself.

Father,
I tremble at the thought of exposing my failures to someone
who could possibly fail me, too. But I realize that in confiding
in others, it produces the humility You want to see in me, as
well as providing a safeguard for my future behavior. Help me
to find other Christian women who are worthy of my trust and
who will help me in the process toward holiness. Thank You
that You hear our prayers and make them effective because of
Your faithfulness.

Heart Reflections

BUILDING FAMILIES OF FAITH

Why, according to James 5:16,
should we confess our sins to
one another?

Why do you think Jesus requires confession in order to promote healing?

Do you think this verse is only referring to physical healing? What else could it mean?

What keeps you from being vulnerable with others? How can you overcome this fear?

Heart of Hearing

So then, my beloved brethren, let every man be swift to hear,
slow to speak, slow to wrath.

JAMES 1:19

My mom had an amazing gift. I relied on it like a flower does the sun. In her company, I found a steady warmth that streamed from her heart—a heart that listened deeply to my hurts and desires, and calmly and patiently nurtured me until I remembered to face the stress in Christ's strength. In retrospect, I realize that on many occasions when I would come home with a certain crisis, she could have easily just told me what to do or put me in my place, frustrated that I had not yet learned my lesson. But she never did. She loved me, instead, through listening and gently leading through kind words of wisdom. The atmosphere of peace she created in our home because of her kindness still draws me back even to this day. It was a haven of hope and love then, and it still is now.

As a mother now myself, I want to remember the silent lessons my mother gave. With four kids constantly working their way into some kind of crisis, my inclination is to swoop down and declare solutions for each. But real peace that produces maturity isn't made that way. It comes through the same, steady patience my mother demonstrated as she trusted Christ to produce His righteousness in me. She knew God would be faithful in His own time, and I hold to that same hope for my children.

As we realize God's hand in every event of our lives, we are freed from the intrinsic need to find immediate solutions, or to get angry when others are slower travelers to truth. Instead, we turn to Him and wait on His timing, because we know it is perfect. And the love that shines in that land of utter dependence warms all the hearts that are blessed enough to walk there.

Father,
I confess to You my tendency toward anger and toward fast solutions instead of seeking first Your face. Forgive me, and help me to take every issue into the consideration of Your Spirit and Your Word. Give me ears that listen and a heart that understands other people's needs. And help me to radiate Your light and love in the moments of crisis to gently lead others to the hope of Christ.

Heart Reflections

BUILDING FAMILIES OF FAITH

Do you know someone who
listens before they speak?

Why do you appreciate that
kind of response?

_____

_____

_____

_____

Are you that kind of wife?
Mother? Why or why not?

_____

_____

_____

_____

Why is it important that we be
quick to listen, but slow to
speak and slow to anger?

_____

_____

_____

_____

_____

Digging for Treasure

Counsel in the heart of man is like deep water, but a man of understanding will draw it out.

PROVERBS 20:5

You know the routine when you run into someone you know:

"Hi! How are you doing?"
"Just fine, thanks. And you?"
"Just great, thanks."

And both parties walk on, still wearing the social smile that everyone expects. It's a conversational exchange we all encounter on a daily basis, and in a way it is a necessary convention to simply acknowledge another person's presence. But in God's economy there is treasure buried beneath the surface of the soul, and it is our obligation and honor as His children to dig until we find it.

It is not that God calls us to painfully deep conversations with every person we talk to. And He's not about us badgering people into an unwanted vulnerability. But a crucial element to relationships that so many Christians miss is the art of asking the right questions—the tool that takes us past pat answers and down into the true caverns of thought that exist below.

I think that this relational pattern has fallen by the wayside for several reasons. Asking requires patience. A willingness to hear whatever the answer may be. And it brings conviction in our own lives. Perhaps that is why Jesus Christ chose to ask so many questions—questions to which He knew the answer. But by asking He gently led others out of their misunderstanding, into the place of His light. As His followers, let us continue in the same manner to lead others out of themselves, and up into Him.

Father,

Thank You for the vast dynamics of body life and Your call for me to tend to all the needs of Your people, not just the ones I casually catch on the surface. Give me wisdom to know when to press forward with questions, and give me the right words that will help draw out the heart thoughts and needs of others. It will require patience, wisdom, and selflessness. I look to You to provide these for me as I humbly obey Your call.

Heart Reflections

BUILDING FAMILIES OF FAITH

Are you satisfied with the depth
of your relationship with your
husband? Your children? Those
around you?

Is it easy or difficult for you to
engage others on a deeper level?
Why or why not?

In your opinion, what effect
does Jesus' questions have on
His listeners?

How can your conversation be
seasoned similarly?

Under the Knife

When I was little, I shuddered at Dad's words: "You know, honey, I'm doing this for your own good." It was his gentle disclaimer before a much more tangible and memorable reinforcement ensued. At the time I didn't understand the depth of his words. Fortunately, the rest of the message rang loud and clear.

It wasn't until I myself became a parent that I fully understood my father's intentions when it came to discipline. His actions really weren't mean, outlandish, or uncalled for. Instead, he provided the necessary rules and rewards that gave my feet direction to walk, while guarding my heart and mind from harmful and wrong influences. Today I often catch myself mouthing the very same words to my children. As far as a heart can be known, I truly want the best for them. My passion keeps me on my feet, correcting, rebuking, consoling, and encouraging my little ones until they can discern truth and act on it by themselves.

But our parental desires pale in comparison to the love and wisdom we find in our heavenly Father. Unlike any earthly experience, He not only knows our actions, but He also knows our heart that motivates them. His discipline is not the result of a book He has read or a reaction to behavior that has caught Him off guard. He knows all things, including the evil that lurks in our hearts. In His sovereign wisdom, He knows exactly what measures it takes to tear out the cancer of our souls and fill them, instead, with new life—His Spirit. As His children we all undergo the knife of this Master Surgeon. Often, the procedure appears painful, discouraging, or pointless. It is then we must trust and submit, knowing that the One who loves us more than we could ever imagine is at work in our lives, making us into healthy, whole children of God. It is my prayer that as you read the following devotionals, you will catch a glimpse of God's radiant light, even if for now the clouds of despair loom dangerously low over your soul. Take heart. God disciplines those whom He loves. In His time the rain will fade, and you will see the warmth of His love as it pours over a changed and triumphant child—you.

Words of Wisdom

If any of you lacks wisdom, let him ask of God, who gives to all liberally and without reproach, and it will be given to him.

JAMES 1:5

When we first moved to our new home in this area, we didn't know much about the community. Finding a good church topped our priority list, and we had aggressively investigated all the churches we could find that we knew would share our beliefs. Though each had its own offerings, neither Thom nor I felt God's peace about any of them. So we continued to pray and pray as the days of the impending delivery of our third child approached.

Then, through a simple conversation with some friends, God handed us the missing piece to the puzzle. They recommended a local church we had not yet tried. By the end of the first service, we knew God had spoken. "This is your new covenant family that I have chosen for you." That same week Winsor was born, along with the news of her heart defect. God's timing could not have been more beautiful, for in our moment of need we knew we had a family of faith waiting to enfold us in their arms and lift our new loved one up to God.

We went to church that following Sunday, and the pastor prayed a prayer of healing over Winsor. God miraculously answered with complete healing. It was a momentous event in my life that let me know just how faithful God is to guide us at the right time, in the right way, when we wait on Him for His wisdom.

Father,

I praise You because You know all things. You hold the past, present, and future in Your hands. I need Your wisdom, Lord, not just for the direction of my life, but also for the direction of my heart toward You. Remind me to turn to You for wisdom, and to wait on You for the right answer.

Heart Reflections

BUILDING FAMILIES OF FAITH

To whom does God give
wisdom according to James 1:5?

What makes us reluctant to
ask?

What are some of the ways
God uses to guide us?

How can this verse eliminate
any anxiety you may have over
a situation?

Grace Multiplied

And above all things have fervent love for one another, for "love will cover a multitude of sins."

1 PETER 4:8

If there's one thing Christians love about God, inevitably it is His gift of forgiveness and His ability to wash us so well that He sees no more trace of the sin that soiled us. We cling to His pardon, count on it, and glory in it. It is our saving grace, and we often thank Him for it.

But an interesting phenomena occurs when other Christians inflict sinful wounds on us. Maybe a friend gossiped behind your back. Your spouse said some deeply hurtful words. Your children rebelled and dishonored your name. It is the side of Christianity where the players who are supposed to be acting out God's love have forgotten their lines and filled them with obscenities instead. It is here, in the fiery furnace of life's disappointments and hurts, that God melts the dross of hypocrisy from our souls. Will we fight back? Will we pretend a forgiveness only to hold a secret grudge? Or will we choose to love the very ones who have intentionally hurt us?

We really don't have any options. If we want to continue in the forgiveness our heavenly Father gives us, then we must walk in His same footsteps—the ones that lead us away from anger, bitterness, and retaliation and take us to His heart of love that hardly notices when others do it wrong. They are big shoes to fill, but His Spirit in us enables us to choose love even in the hardest circumstance. By our love our offenders will see Christ. And in Christ they, too, will learn to love and forgive others.

Father,

I am so grateful for Your faithful forgiveness. You require nothing from me but a repentant heart, which I gladly give to You. Forgive me for holding others accountable for their wrongs to me. Help me to love them the way that You do; when they hurt me, help me to extend to them the same unconditional forgiveness that You have shown me.

Heart Reflections

BUILDING FAMILIES OF FAITH

Why does God want us to love "above all things"?

What does the verse mean
when it says that "love will
cover a multitude of sins"?

How does Christ's life
demonstrate this principle?

Who do you need to forgive?
How can you show that person
true love?

Good Grief

Now no chastening seems to be joyful for the present, but painful;
nevertheless, afterward it yields the peaceable fruit of righteousness
to those who have been trained by it.

HEBREWS 12:11

I was in the prime of my life. As yet unencumbered with children, I was busy about Thom's growing business and our ministry. Needless to say, it completely caught me off guard when I ruptured a disc in my back, leaving me helpless and in constant, excruciating pain. Not wanting to slow my pace, we immediately sought out doctors, chiropractors—everyone we could think of to remedy the problem. Nothing worked. Hopeless, we looked to God for help.

My prayers reflected the character growth God was nurturing in my heart during this time of crisis. Initially, I begged and pleaded for Him to take away my pain and restore my health. But the more I prayed, the more I realized that I didn't just need healing. I needed Him— to depend on Him and need only Him. Slowly my prayers shifted from, "Lord, do what I want" to "Lord,

Your will be done." Healing became secondary to the hope of knowing Him better. As I yielded to His work in my life, God met me in the midst of my pain. Thankfully, in His time, He led us to just the right doctor. Not only did God heal my heart, but He enabled the doctor to restore my back to wholeness through one simple surgery.

It is a lesson I carry with me every day of my life. I know that each moment of my life comes from the loving hand of God, and all things must work together for my good because I belong to Him. Our challenge is to not receive God's discipline (life's trials) as something to conquer or quell, but as a means to surrendering our souls even more, that we might be drawn ever deeper into His heart.

Father,
No one likes pain, especially me. And I shudder to think that
You sometimes use painful things in life to point me to You.
But I know that Your grace is sufficient for me, and You do not
send anything my way that is too much for me to bear. Teach
me, Lord, to seek Your face in the midst of every moment,
knowing that You use these trials to cultivate Christ's
character in me.

Heart Reflections

BUILDING FAMILIES OF FAITH

How does God train His

children in righteousness?

Why do you think that the process is often painful?

Where must our focus remain during life's trials? Why?

How does our attitude toward discipline affect its outcome in our lives?

Image Issues

For You formed my inward parts; You covered me in my mother's womb. I will praise You, for I am fearfully and wonderfully made; marvelous are Your works, and that my soul knows very well.

PSALM 139:13, 14

Thom's fame is no secret. At times, it seems as if all he touches turns to gold, and I marvel at the miraculous giftings he has been given. And as a part of his family, we all share a portion of his special ministry. But Thom is not the only person designed with purpose. Each of us, including myself, must come to realize our identity in Christ and what our own special calling is that God has given us.

When we begin to doubt our distinction in life, we must remember the root of our existence. Before we were ever born, God knew about us. He designed us exactly the way we needed to be to walk in His perfect will for us. It is not a matter of achievements, for those may or may not stack up according to the world's standards. But what counts is the character that comes in the midst of trying.

In essence, it is the art of being and becoming the very person God created you to be. There simply is no such thing as a lesser life when we walk in what God has laid out for us.

We are all unique—a special part of God's deliberate plan to drive us to dependence on Him and to delight in the incredible creativity of it all. It is a wonderful thing to be handwrought by the world's Creator. Instead of complaining or second-guessing Him, let's celebrate our differences and seek out our special purpose in Him.

Father,
Thank You for making me exactly the way You chose to make
me. Forgive me for complaining about Your design. I ask that,
instead, You give me the wisdom I need to surrender my
perceived shortcomings to You, that You may miraculously use
them for Your glory and the advancement of Your kingdom.
Help me, too, to see the beauty of Your plan in the other
members of Christ's body, the church, and help me to
encourage them accordingly.

Heart Reflections

BUILDING FAMILIES OF FAITH

When did God first know about you?

Why is it wrong for us to reject
or insult others or ourselves?

What makes us special?

How can we celebrate our
differences?

Court Recess

For I know of nothing against myself, yet I am not justified by this;
but He who judges me is the Lord. Therefore judge nothing before
the time, until the Lord comes, who will both bring to light the
hidden things of darkness and reveal the counsels of the hearts.
Then each one's praise will come from God.

1 CORINTHIANS 4:4, 5

We call it women's intuition. Men understand it as the despicable art of attaching moods or meanings to otherwise benign words. It is the paradox of women's virtues—the ability to perceive hidden relational needs and implications, but it also brings the possibility of misperceived intentions and sinful judgment.

Fortunately, for Christians, we have a way to win in both situations. Under the Spirit's control, we can use our God-given insight to understand needs our spouse, our children, or others may not even know they have. We can spot bitterness in its beginning stages and address it to help dig it out. We can identify discouragement and send a timely word of praise. We can even sense dissension and work to reestablish right relationships in our lives.

But let us take Paul's warning to heart, too—for there is nothing to be misunderstood here. While we use our gifts for good, let us not get in the habit of interpreting other people's intentions in a negative light. In 1 Corinthians 13 God tells us that true love "thinks no evil," and it "bears all things, believes all things, hopes all things, endures all things." When we begin to assume that other people's actions originate out of bad motives, then we have declared ourselves a judge instead of one who loves. Only God knows the heart, and we must leave the ruling to the One who rightly wears the robe.

Father,

There is a fine line between discernment and judgment.
The first You have called me to apply, while the latter is reserved for only You. Thank You for giving me wisdom in my relationships, Lord, and I pray that You would help me to rightly perceive the inner needs of those around me. But guard my heart against false accusations and needless hurt. Help me to see everything through Your eyes of love.

Heart Reflections

BUILDING FAMILIES OF FAITH

Are you guilty of an overly

sensitive or critical spirit?

Explain.

Why is it easier to assume the
worst of others instead of the
best?

What makes us think we can
know another person's heart?

What is the difference between
discernment and judgment?

How can you love wisely while
leaving judging up to God?

Panic or Peace?

Be anxious for nothing, but in everything by prayer and supplication, with thanksgiving, let your requests be made known to God; and the peace of God, which surpasses all understanding, will guard your hearts and minds through Christ Jesus.

PHILIPPIANS 4:6, 7

If the trials are particularly tough, trusting God tends to be easier for me. Bad health. Career crisis. Rejection. These are trying times, indeed—but they fall so far above my control that it is easier to commit them to the Lord and rest in His will. All I can do in these situations is pray anyway, and the peace that the Lord promises inevitably comes.

My battle rages more on the field of trivialities—where Thom seems overloaded with deadlines, my house rocks under the chaos of rowdy kids, and my list of to-dos grows beyond the doable. I seem to sweat the small stuff, because in my mind—these things are my domain, my responsibility, and my fault if I fail to do them. Somewhere in my mental compartment God is relegated to the big and important events, while I flounder around in the daily details that drag me down in stress and despair.

When the Spirit is leading, I can detect my distraction from a godly focus. As Bill Bright suggests in one of his recent books, I "breathe out" all the events that are stressing me out, and I breathe in the reality of God's sovereignty (even in the details) and simply relax. It requires not only identifying my mental state, but also excusing myself from the fray that is causing it—if only for a moment—to refocus on Christ. When I do let my requests be made known to God, the same peace that pervades my soul in the serious crises comes over me in the midst of my mundane day and prepares my heart to joyfully handle every trial and triumph God brings my way.

Father,

I am always amazed to remember that You not only control all things, but You care about them, too. When I am bogged down under stress, You care. And You have made provision for my peace and rest. Teach me how to enter that place of peace, and fill me with Your discerning Spirit that I may remain in an attitude of prayer throughout the day, giving each detail to You so that I can calmly walk in Your truth.

Heart Reflections

BUILDING FAMILIES OF FAITH

What stresses you out the most? Why?

Why should we be thankful in
trying times?

What does God promise to do
if we turn it over to Him?

What are some practical ways
to remember Philippians 4:6, 7
throughout the day?

Keys to the Kingdom

But seek first the kingdom of God and His righteousness, and all these things shall be added to you.

MATTHEW 6:33

When Thom and I began work on our ministry we had one main goal: to know Christ and share that hope with the world. It started with little more than Thom's vision, talent, and prayers, but we proceeded in faith that we were following God's leading. Now, more than 18 years later, we are witnesses to God's abounding faithfulness and overwhelming provision for our family not just financially, but physically, spiritually, and emotionally as well. It is a new position in life, far from the history of financial and spiritual poverty we hold in many ways.

But despite the extravagant blessings, our goal remains firm. Even in the midst of an overtly affluent community we are committed to seeking first God's kingdom. Everything else we need God promises to add unto us (as He does for all of His children) in His perfect time. The truth is, fame, finances, and the pleasures of this world come and go, but His kingdom is established forever. It is the safest and surest investment Christians can make, for the returns are richer than anything the world has to offer.

We were born to love God and enjoy Him forever. By making Him our highest pursuit, we are satisfied in the very deepest recesses of our souls. No matter what our socioeconomic status may be, as Christians and coheirs with Christ, we experience the wealth of knowing Christ's peace and purpose for our lives. Let whatever else life holds come as it may because God is good, and our lives are linked to eternal prosperity in Him.

Father,
The riches this world offers are alluring. I crave comfort and
stability, and I confess that I often seek it in the wrong places.
You have told me to seek You first and trust You to provide
everything else I need. By faith I do trust You and rejoice that
You are my portion forever. May Your kingdom come and
Your will be done on earth as it is in heaven. Thank You for
letting me be a part of it, and for Your promise to always
protect and provide for me.

Heart Reflections

BUILDING FAMILIES OF FAITH

What exactly is the kingdom of God?

What does it mean to seek it
first?

What are some warning signs
that you are not seeking it first?

What does God promise to do
if we obey Him?

Let Freedom Sing

There is therefore now no condemnation to those who are in Christ Jesus, who do not walk according to the flesh, but according to the Spirit. For the law of the Spirit of life in Christ Jesus has made me free from the law of sin and death.

ROMANS 8:1, 2

We must admit it. Sometimes it just makes us feel better about ourselves if we wallow around in the misery of our sin for awhile. We entertain thoughts like, "I can't come to God now, not after all I've done." Or, "Maybe if I'm miserable long enough for my mistake, then God will forgive me and love me again." Satan loves this stuff, because he knows it is just the wrong perspective that keeps us from growing in Christ.

Swing the pendulum to the other extreme and you encounter the legalism and lovelessness that characterizes so many Christian lives. Either for fear of failure or in an attempt at outward righteousness, they construct rules stricter than God's own guidelines, building a façade of holiness that is devoid of God's true Spirit.

God's Word says differently. Throw off your shroud of morbid introspection and futile attempts at self-righteousness. We didn't earn God's salvation by our performance, and we won't achieve sanctification by it either. We begin by faith and we continue to walk in it with Christ for the rest of our lives. Be gone sour faces! Get lost gloomy spirits! Victory is ours through our Lord Jesus Christ! Because of Him, we have no condemnation. We have nothing left but to rejoice in God our Savior!

Father,
I fall on my knees in humble recognition of Your saving grace.
You have called me to Yourself. You have provided the
atonement for my sins—for all of time. In You alone I find
favor, worth, and true joy. Thank You, thank You, thank You
that You have made me Your child. Help me to identify Satan's
attempts to distract me from the simple truth of trusting in
Jesus for my hope of glory.

Heart Reflections

BUILDING FAMILIES OF FAITH

Who is no longer under

condemnation?

Why aren't we?

What does it mean to walk
according to the flesh? The
Spirit?

How can we walk in the
victory that Christ says is ours
through Him?

Fighting Fatigue

Come to Me, all you who labor and are heavy laden, and I will give you rest. Take My yoke upon you and learn from Me, for I am gentle and lowly in heart, and you will find rest for your souls.

MATTHEW 11:28, 29

It isn't as difficult for me now. Early in the morning before the children rise, or somewhere in the middle of the day when they are away at school, I set aside a little time just for me. Curled up with a hot cup of tea, I gaze at Thom's oversized original work, "Beyond Autumn Gates," and mentally enter into that realm of peace he so beautifully paints in the picture. It is my moment for reflection, for recuperation, for a little R and R. And Christian women—we need it!

Every life has different seasons, and in the interest of our sanity it is important that we recognize them. When children are very young, physical fatigue is intense and the emotional drain at its deepest. But time will pass, and the children will grow. Soon, more opportunities will come when you can actually get away—if only for a few minutes—to remember who you are, whose you are, and what your purpose is. Refocused and refreshed, we are then able to face the day renewed in Christ's strength.

Jesus' rest is not an optimistic option. It is required for our souls to stay strong that we may fight the good fight all the way to the end. If you feel tired physically, emotionally, spiritually, then stop for a moment. As Jesus often did, pull away from the throng to sit at the Father's feet and receive from Him the love you need to continue. Take a nap. Put off laundry long enough for a simple walk. Don't be afraid to ask your spouse or a friend for help. But take Jesus up on His offer. He hears your cry and welcomes you to come to Him for rest.

Father,
I am tired and torn in too many directions. Sleep seems so far
away from my body and soul. I need Your strength. I need
Your Spirit's fire to fuel my soul. Help me to weed out of my
life all the things that are superfluous to Your will for me.
Teach me to make the most of my time and to take aside a
portion of it to receive attention from You alone. Thank
You for Your promise of rest. Help me to realize its
importance in my life.

Heart Reflections

BUILDING FAMILIES OF FAITH

Would you describe your life as peaceful or harried? Why?

What kind of rest is Jesus talking about in verse 29?

How does Jesus provide "soul rest"?

How can simply understanding Christ's provision for you invoke true rest?

Shine On

Like stars in a velvet black sky, their light still shines. It reaches across the chasm of time and culture to connect then and now in a miraculous way. They are the precious jewels in God's treasure chest of truth. They are the women of the Bible and their lives humbly, dramatically, eternally illuminate God's special love for all of His little girls.

Just as diamonds don't shine on their own but reflect the radiance of white light as a prism of glorious color, so these women glowed with a glory not their own. Their beauty came from God who meticulously, lovingly, and thoughtfully removed the hardened and black coal from their souls and handcrafted lives that shone His love and truth from every angle.

It is a blessing to be able to see these gems of truth so beautifully hidden throughout Scripture's pages. Each time we encounter one of these precious women of God, we are reminded of His grace, His love, and His plan of prosperity and hope for His people. Be encouraged as you read, dear Sisters, and be reminded of the special place you hold in the heart of our heavenly Father. He sees you and knows you, too, just as He beheld these women so many years ago. Though life's refining fires may burn brightly, He holds the flame—and your life—in His loving hands. And as the dross of sin melts away, He is pleased to reveal the beauty of His Son, the radiance of God, in you. May your own life become a mirror image of God's glory, a testimony of grace that shines for all ages to come.

The First Lady

*So God created man in His own image; in the image of God He
created him; male and female He created them. Then God blessed
them, and God said to them, "Be fruitful and multiply; fill the earth
and subdue it; have dominion over the fish of the sea, over the birds
of the air, and over every living thing that moves on the earth."*

GENESIS 1:27, 28

Children are a tremendous blessing. They bring joy,
innocence, and new life to our souls. It is impossible to
let a day go by without tousling their hair or kissing their
cheeks and gazing at them in awed amazement. After all,
they are our kids, and kids are a good thing.

But for marriage there is something even better. God
knew it, and soon Adam did, too. When God realized
that Adam was lonely and needed someone, it is
interesting to note that God did not give him children.
He gave man woman, the feminine counterpart to man's
created image of God. Eve was the First Lady of all
creation, and in the pattern of marriage God established
from the beginning, man and woman enjoyed intimacy
and joint-rule over the rest of creation.

Thom and I had six years before children to enjoy life together as soul mates, the "makers" of our own little world. And even now that four children fill our home, we have not forgotten the love, passion, and companionship we cultivated before the others came. We guard it carefully, making certain that we spend time alone on dates, business excursions, or just time to talk each night after the kids go to bed. Christian women, we must watch ourselves, that we do not reverse God's order of priorities. Keep your husband's needs at the top, and from there work diligently to see that other family members' needs are met. If you do, your children will see a biblical portrait of God's provision for them, and your family will grow all the stronger because of it.

Father,
I admit that I think my husband can fend for himself while the
clamor of my children's needs sounds louder in my ears. But
when I neglect him, I am forgetting my call as First Lady of
the home, to help my husband be the best leader he can be.
Forgive my indiscretion, and help me to realize the ways I can
best support and respect my husband while also tending to the
children. Only by Your grace is the right balance possible, and I
come before Your throne now to receive it.

Heart Reflections

BUILDING FAMILIES OF FAITH

In whose image was woman made?

From what did God make her?

How does her creation symbolize God's intended union in marriage?

How can you be a better helper to your husband?

Star Light

"For if you remain completely silent at this time, relief and deliverance will arise for the Jews from another place, but you and your father's house will perish. Yet who knows whether you have come to the kingdom for such a time as this?" Then Esther told them to reply to Mordecai: "Go, gather all the Jews who are present in Shushan, and fast for me; neither eat nor drink for three days, night or day. My maids and I will fast likewise. And so I will go to the king, which is against the law; and if I perish, I perish!"

ESTHER 4:14–16

In the midst of captivity, a star was born. Esther, whose name means "star," relied on God's strength and sovereignty to set her own people free from an insidious enemy of the Jewish people. Because of her faith in God, she braved the consequences of breaking the law to approach the king and appeal to his mercy. God honored her obedience and blessed her by not only saving her people, but also by crowning her queen—even in the midst of captivity.

Esther's light of faith still shines through the ages right into our worlds, too. God never guarantees us a good environment. In fact, it is often in the harshest scenarios that God's light shines the brightest in us. When Thom and I first got married, we lived in a low-rent apartment located beside an alcoholic and above some drug dealers. I worked the night shift as an RN, so Thom changed his schedule to reflect mine. The times were tough from a financial and fatigue standpoint, but where environment failed, love and fun times flourished. We'd take bike rides at two A.M., or moonlit walks just to squeeze in some time together. God showed us both that He is Lord and full of abundant life, whatever our station in life seems to be.

Like Esther, we can rise above our surroundings and step out in obedient faith because God is faithful. When others around you crumble under circumstances, they will see your unwavering strength and be led to the source—the love and light of Christ.

Father,
Thank You for Esther's encouragement for Christians to trust
You even in the darkest times. I know that You have a reason
for placing me exactly where I am right now in life. Help me
to not only see Your hand in it, but to walk in the works You
have prepared for me here and now. I rejoice in my
circumstances, good or bad, because I know they come from
Your loving hand, and Your gentle Spirit will not leave me
here, but lead me home.

Heart Reflections

BUILDING FAMILIES OF FAITH

Have you ever lived or worked
in undesirable circumstances?
Explain.

_____

_____

_____

_____

_____

What was your attitude toward
it/God during that time?

_____

_____

_____

How can God use difficult
circumstances to draw us to
Him and reveal His glory?

How did Esther regard her
own life in light of obeying
God?

What attitude toward God
must we have to be able to rise
above our circumstances?

Ruby of Redemption

*And she said, "Look, your sister-in-law has gone back to her people
and to her gods; return after your sister-in-law." But Ruth said:
"Entreat me not to leave you, or to turn back from following after
you; for wherever you go, I will go; and wherever you lodge, I will
lodge; your people shall be my people, and your God, my God."*

RUTH 1:15, 16

It was Ruth's darkest hour. Her husband, provider, and
friend was dead. Her sister-in-law's husband shared the
same fate. To everyone around her, it seemed clear that
God had spoken, and what He had to say was more
horrible than what any woman could bear. Three women,
Naomi, Ruth, and Orpah, were now husbandless,
childless, and utterly hopeless. Naomi reckoned it to be
harsh judgment from God. Orpah reconsidered her faith
and ultimately abandoned it in hopes of finding a better
future with her familiar people and gods. But Ruth's
newfound faith stood firm. Instead of despair, she clung
to the one sure hope she had—a foreign people and their
foreign God whom she had come to know as Father.

Even more beautiful than the portrait of faithful loyalty
Ruth lived out was the remarkable unveiling of God's own
faithfulness to His children—even the ones like Ruth who

had been grafted in from a distant land. What had begun as a tragedy turned to triumph in the hands of the all-sovereign God who led Naomi and Ruth right into the fields of a nearby relative (a rich one, at that). Through simple steps of obedience Ruth received this man's favor and soon became his wife. The shame and sorrow of widowhood was replaced with a wealth beyond her wildest imaginations, including a godly husband and eventually a child who would become grandfather to King David.

Dear sisters, many events in life may look like only needless tragedies, but take heart. Our God is the same God whom Ruth followed. We, too, look forward to a promising future because we trust the One who holds it in His hand. Though the times now may seem bitter, wait for Him. He promises to turn everything that comes to us for our good, and will shower the sweetness of His love on us in due season.

Father,
It seems to me that life would just be better altogether if I never had to encounter trying times. But in Your wisdom, You use the pain of life to lead us to even deeper pleasure found only in You. Help me to trust You in the moments of crisis, and to calmly take Your hand as You lead me through unchartered lands into more bountiful blessing.

Heart Reflections

BUILDING FAMILIES OF FAITH

Why did Orpah turn back?

Why did Ruth remain with
Naomi?

How did God bless Ruth's
obedience?

How can we know God will
bless us, too, if we persevere in
Him?

Heaven's Laughter

*And the L*ORD *visited Sarah as He had said, and the L*ORD *did for Sarah as He had spoken. For Sarah conceived and bore Abraham a son in his old age, at the set time of which God had spoken to him. . . . And Sarah said, "God has made me laugh, and all who hear will laugh with me."*

GENESIS 21:1, 2, 6

It can happen to us, too. Of course, we probably won't bear children after we are in our senior years (and I doubt many of us want that anyway), but we can share Sarah's laugh. We can throw down our pretenses, worries, concerns, responsibilities—everything that bows our shoulders under its unruly burden—and let out an exultant shout of relief. Dance like David. Sing like Solomon. And laugh like Sarah, for she finally came to see the sovereignty of God and rested in the joyous shade of His provision.

I think that much of the reason behind Christianity's often perceived sour face is the failure to recognize God's control in all the details of life. We take responsibility meant for Him and reel under its weight until the joy in Christ cannot be found. In truth, though, we do not have the ability to impact eternity on our own. We only have hope, purpose, and meaning in Christ because of Him. Thom and I have even adopted an attitude that helps with this perspective: When we are faced with a potentially stressful or difficult situation, we ask, "What's the worst possible scenario that can come of this?" The answer is, of course, death. But for the Christian, even death holds glory because of our ensuing home in heaven. Since life and death are both win-win situations for God's children, we are freed to relax and revel in the joyous and abundant life that comes from living in Christ.

Father,
I want to laugh like Sarah. I want to throw caution to the
wind and recklessly rest in Your divine grace and love for me.
Thank You that You are trustworthy and powerful to do all
that You will in my life. Help me to face life's trials with a
true faith that finds anchor in Your ability and joy
in Your perfect plan.

Heart Reflections

BUILDING FAMILIES OF FAITH

Why do you think God waited until Sarah was old to give her a child?

Is there any hope or dream of
yours for which you are still
waiting?

How does knowing that God is
in control help build patience
and confidence?

Is your spirit heavy with
concerns? List any burdens
here and leave them before
the throne of God who alone
holds the power to lift them.

The Harlot Heroine

By faith the harlot Rahab did not perish with those who did not believe, when she had received the spies with peace.

HEBREWS 11:31

It must have been unnerving to know that she and her family must stand alone. To choose God meant losing the life she had always known, the friends and families who had made Jericho her home. By God's grace, Rahab understood the truth, and she knew that salvation stemmed from it—from Him—alone. So she stood alone, clinging to the hope of grace. Though the world came crashing down around her, she and her family were saved.

God knows it is not easy to be alone. That is why He promised to never leave us nor forsake us, and He encourages us to take comfort in the knowledge of His presence. Are you alone? Not just in terms of numbers, but do you feel as if the loved ones around you are lost in sin and reject God's loving call on their lives? Look at Rahab then, and lift your spirits. The same God who called a harlot to repentance and led her to redemption cannot only take care of you, but can lead the lost to Himself as well. Thom and I both have witnessed this miracle of grace in our families, first with Thom's father, who came to the Lord at age 75, and later my grandmother at age 81. It was simply a matter of praying, waiting, and watching God at work over the years.

Be patient, dear sisters, as you wait for God's salvation—not only for yourself but for others, as well. Like Rahab, your commitment to truth and concern for your family may be the connecting link to Christ for them. So take heart. Cling to the Rock of truth. In God's time He may use you, too, to pull others from the path of destruction to His sure foundation.

Father,
Thank You that I am never truly alone. You promise to be
with me always. Thank You, too, that You see me in my
situation now, and You care about me and my loved ones. I
commit myself and them to You, Father, and pray that in Your
time You would lead us into Your everlasting arms of love.
Help me to have Rahab's faith, to forsake all that might seem
comfortable for the true and lasting pleasure of knowing You.

Heart Reflections

BUILDING FAMILIES OF FAITH

Of everyone in Jericho, why do you think God chose Rahab, a harlot, to save?

What did Rahab lose by choosing God?

What did she gain?

How can her story encourage you to trust and wait on the Lord for salvation?

Good, Better, Best

But Martha was distracted with much serving, and she approached Him and said, "Lord, do You not care that my sister has left me to serve alone? Therefore tell her to help me." And Jesus answered and said to her, "Martha, Martha, you are worried and troubled about many things. But one thing is needed, and Mary has chosen that good part, which will not be taken away from her."

LUKE 10:40–42

Ouch! Just when Martha thought the Teacher would soothe her hurts, He poured in the salt of truth instead. But Jesus' gentle rebuke to His overburdened sister was not born out of callousness, but birthed from a heart that sought to heal her wounds at the very core. To Martha, her dilemma was simple. There were dishes to bake, tables to prepare, pots to wash, and she couldn't do it all by herself. If the truth were known, she probably looked on Mary's lack of activity as mere laziness and resented her for it. Martha's cure? Get to work. But Jesus' answer? Get to worship!

For performance-oriented souls this is the last secret to Christian service they want to hear. It slows down what they consider to be kingdom progress—a hierarchy of to-dos with an enormity so grand most mortals would simply faint under the weight. So they dare not slow—and certainly not stop—to sit even at Christ's feet, lest they be overtaken by their own Christian burden.

For all the Marthas who still work in the church, teetering on the edge of burnout, Jesus' call to you is clear. Service is good, and it will be rewarded. But there is something better. Lay your burdens down at Christ's feet, and rest your souls under His care. Receive from Him everlasting life, and replenish your spirit with His living water. Like Mary, listen to Him. Receive from Him. In His time you will accomplish His work, as He leads you to do it. This time it will be done in His strength. Resentment will turn to rejoicing. And His love will light the way.

Father,
I think I feel more spiritual when I can see that I am
accomplishing things for Your kingdom. But the anger, fatigue,
and burnout lurking in my soul betrays my motives to earn
Your approval instead of resting in the reality that You love me
completely already. Help me to believe that Your greatest desire
for me is to spend time with You. And when I do meet You in
that quiet place, please change my heart that my life might be a
pleasing sacrifice of service to You.

Heart Reflections
BUILDING FAMILIES OF FAITH

Why is it easier to "do things" for God rather than spend time with Him?

Do you feel distracted from the
Lord? Why or why not?

Describe one of your most
intimate moments with the
Savior.

What can you do to turn your
quiet times into true moments
of listening and worship?

Miraculous Makeover

Now when He rose early on the first day of the week, He appeared first to Mary Magdalene, out of whom He had cast seven demons.

MARK 16:9

Americans are fascinated with makeovers. From the Cinderella story to syndicated T.V. talk shows, we want to know what it is like to be transformed from the terribly mundane or ugly into a glorious beauty. We know it is superficial, yet somehow we feel drawn—almost mesmerized—by the process. Despite its apparent shallowness, I believe the drive comes from somewhere deeper. It bubbles up from the recesses of our souls that wonder whether or not anything can be salvaged of us and made into something beautiful to behold.

Mary Magdalene probably wondered the same thing. After all, when Jesus found her she was possessed by seven different demons. It doesn't get much worse than that. Undaunted, Jesus delivered her from spiritual death and directed her into the loving arms of the heavenly Father. Throughout the Gospel commentaries, Mary's name continues to crop up in even the most dangerous situations. She had seen the Master at work. Her makeover was more than skin deep. It went straight to her soul, and she would never be the same.

It is interesting that Jesus chose to appear first to this same Mary after His resurrection from the dead. He didn't reserve it for the more glamorous or admired apostle. He reserved His glory for a formerly demon-possessed woman, a devoted follower who found her hope alone in the Christ she adored. Her life asserts it, but Christ's appearance confirms it. Our past does not present a problem to God. Instead, He lives to resurrect our dead hearts, free us from bondage, and create in us an unsurpassable beauty that surges from His love in us.

Father,
Thank You for the tremendous gift of forgiveness. I often think
of my failures and fear they will separate me from You, but
that is a lie from Satan that I must reject. You have separated
me from my sins as far as the east is from the west, and You
consider me beautiful in Your sight. Thank You, precious Lord,
for Your power to transform lives into an everlasting work
of art. Thank You, too, for Your work in my heart—
the miraculous makeover from destitute sinner to a
cherished child of God.

Heart Reflections

BUILDING FAMILIES OF FAITH

What do you think drove

Mary's devotion to Christ?

How does understanding forgiveness expand our ability to love?

Is anything beyond Christ's ability to forgive?

How does this knowledge encourage you to pursue Christ wholeheartedly?

A Perfect Picture

Charm is deceitful and beauty is passing, but a woman who fears the Lord, she shall be praised.

PROVERBS 31:30

From day one I knew I was outmatched. Thom's numerous talents, artistic gifts notwithstanding, outshone my average abilities in a glaring way. Quickly I learned God's lesson that comparison in any form is sin, because He blesses, gifts, and requires from the members of His body different things. As our minds stay focused on Him, He produces the work in us that He wants done, whether or not it appears glamorous to the world.

It has been a most rewarding and relaxing lesson indeed, particularly when I approach the famous Proverbs 31 text in Scripture. For many Christian women this portrait of the ideal godly woman is more of a frustration than an encouragement because of its seemingly unattainable standard of perfection. But what we need to remember is that the picture Solomon paints for us in these verses truly is perfect, for it describes the life of a woman who is fully yielded to the Lord. For each of us the list of attributes and accomplishments might be different. But a heart that is filled with the Holy Spirit overflows in attitudes and works like the Proverbs 31 woman. Apart from Christ her standard is too high for anyone. But with Christ all things are possible.

So let Christ work in your heart. Submit to His direction as He convicts of sin, encourages you toward obedience, and ever gently leads you closer to His heart. It is this intimacy that fueled the passion of the Proverbs woman, and it is the only way to become the woman God longs for you to be.

Father,
Thank You that You do not ask of me more than I can give.
The Proverbs 31 woman standard is high, even as Christ's
perfection is unattainable by sinful man. But through Christ's
atoning work in my heart, You can produce a life that reflects
Your glory, power, energy, and love. Change my heart, Lord,
that I might make the most of every opportunity to live in a
way that is pleasing to You and is in accordance with Your
calling on my life.

Heart Reflections

BUILDING FAMILIES OF FAITH

What does it mean to "fear the Lord"?

Why does God desire this above works?

How does fearing God lead to good works?

What are ways to cultivate the fear of the Lord in your heart?

God's Graciousness

And Hannah prayed and said: "My heart rejoices in the LORD; my horn is exalted in the LORD. I smile at my enemies, because I rejoice in Your salvation."

1 SAMUEL 2:1

The priest thought she was drunk. Fists clenched, tears streaming, face heavenward, Hannah silently poured out her heart to the Lord. Her hope was in God, and her heart was true—yet at the same time her heart was broken. She longed to feel the warmth of a newborn baby in her arms. To see an extension of herself in the eyes of her own child. But Hannah was barren, and she had come to lay the shame and disappointment at her Savior's feet in exchange for hope.

It was not long before Hannah discovered the true meaning of her own name, "Graciousness," for God revealed it to her in a special way. Almost a year later, Samuel was born, a firstborn son full of promise, his mother's pride and joy. But the biggest miracle, I believe, is this: In her moment of despair, Hannah saw God's grace. In her moment of glory, she remembered God's favor and freely gave back to God what He had given to her—new life. Keeping her promise, when Samuel was of age she turned him over to Eli for work in the tabernacle. She knew now that God had shone His face on her, loved her, and longed for her to find contentment solely in Him.

What does your heart yearn for? Financial security? A boyfriend? A strong marriage? Children? Like Hannah, lay your hopes before God's throne of grace, and receive what He has in store for you. But remember to receive with an open hand, for all that we have belongs only to Him. He is the One to whom we cling, and with our hopes set in Him we will never be disappointed.

Father,
I do have strong desires that may or may not be a part of Your
will for me. Give me wisdom to know what and how to ask,
and to humbly trust You that You will provide the very best for
me in Your time. Help me not to forget Your grace, and to
always receive with an open hand for You to move
freely in my life.

Heart Reflections

BUILDING FAMILIES OF FAITH

For what does your heart

yearn?

What is your heart attitude if
God chooses to withhold it?

Why does God delay or
withhold things from His
children sometimes?

Why is it important that we be
completely content in Him
alone?

Eden Revisited

I am my beloved's, and my beloved is mine.

SONG OF SOLOMON 6:3

It is evening, and the last child has been tucked into bed. I breathe a sigh of relief and walk past a host of chores waiting with a defiant air to be done. There will be time enough later for that. Now, it's our time.

Thom has beaten me out onto our patio, his feet already propped up on the table, as he gazes up at the stars. "Hi, hon," he greets me, as I take my usual place and kick my feet up next to his. We soak in the moment, the silence, and slowly begin our nightly talk. Earlier in our marriage, we used to keep what we called a "glowbook" where we wrote down the exciting events of the day so that we wouldn't forget to tell the other one about it. Now, after 18 years of marriage, the "glow" is innate, and Thom and I find it easy to spend hours talking together. It is a precious time for both of us, the fuel that fires our passionate marriage after so many years. No T.V. No computers. No phone interruptions. Just us. And our love is blazing hotter and brighter now than ever before.

Sound like the garden of Eden? In a way it is a return to the original pattern of relating, where Christ is central and two creatures of grace gather around to celebrate the passion and love God intends for husband and wife. Even though our sin does affect the picture, Christ's pardon makes it possible to look beyond imperfections to the hope of glory both husband and wife share. Our mate, next to Christ, is our most precious gift from God. As Solomon said, "I am my beloved's, and my beloved is mine." Protect the beautiful covenant that binds you together. Nurture it. Honor it. And experience a love that will last all your days.

Father,
Thank You for the beautiful picture of love You paint for us
through the words of Solomon and the Shulamite woman. It
really seems too good to be true that You want me to have that
kind of passion and love in my marriage, but You wouldn't
have devoted an entire book to it if it weren't possible or
important. Help me to set aside distractions to focus solely on
my mate, and help me to look for ways to encourage him,
spend time with him, and love him with a passion that grows
with each passing day.

Heart Reflections

BUILDING FAMILIES OF FAITH

Is your husband your best
earthly friend? Why or why
not?

What do you allow to distract
you from your devotion to him?

Why do you think God
included the Song of Solomon
in the Bible?

How can you begin to build
passion into your own
marriage?

Silent Service

And all those who heard it marveled at those things which were
told them by the shepherds. But Mary kept all these things and
pondered them in her heart.

LUKE 2:18, 19

She could have demanded explanations. Alternatives. Or at least a say in the proceedings. But instead, Mary pondered in her heart the miraculous provision of God inside her womb and humbly accepted God's will for her life. She saw the call as an opportunity to serve, a sacrifice to God of simple obedience.

Oh, that women today would glean from Mary's wisdom instead of the ways of the world! Unfortunately, we are often bombarded with self-centered ideology cloaked in feminism. Worldly rationale says to serve ourselves first—and to fight for our rights to dictate, dominate, and deviate from God's Word to best suit ourselves. The arguments are so compelling and appealing to our sinful nature that even grounded Christian women waver in the right perspective. But it need not be so. Simply remember Mary, the woman God chose to mother His Son. She surrendered all that she had to serve the Savior. She gave up herself, but in the end, gained Christ. And that is our right, our highest privilege as Christians. Like Mary, we empty ourselves that we might be filled with the life of Christ and, by so doing, we open the opportunity for visitors near and far to worship the King.

Father,
You have clearly said in Your Word that You value a gentle
and quiet spirit. It allows You to speak and enables me to hear.
It also softens others around me. But despite benefits of
obedience, I find in my heart a rebellious spirit that does not
want to sacrifice my selfish desires. I confess it, repent, and ask
for You to change me and make even me a woman who
quietly, gently, rests my soul in You.

Heart Reflections

BUILDING FAMILIES OF FAITH

Why do you think God chose
Mary to mother His Son?

*What are the qualities of a
gentle and quiet spirit?*

*Why is the concept of
submission to God, your
husband, or others so difficult?*

*How does Mary's example
encourage us to live as
Christian women?*

Holy Heritage

I thank God, whom I serve with a pure conscience, as my
forefathers did, as without ceasing I remember you in my prayers
night and day . . . when I call to remembrance the genuine faith
that is in you, which dwelt first in your grandmother Lois and your
mother Eunice, and I am persuaded is in you also.

2 TIMOTHY 1:3, 5

Standing on the edge of the walkway, you find yourself still waving. The car full of college-bound kids, including your "baby" is now out of sight. They were so happy, and for that you are glad. But inside your soul you suppress a strange fear and surrounding sadness. When you closed the car door with your child inside, you knew you had closed—forever—a chapter in your life that had come to seem as life itself.

But when you face that closure, remember this: Throughout the many stages of life and growth, God never closes the door on communicating His truths to our children. Fortunately for Timothy, his mother and grandmother continued to faithfully teach their child and grandchild the truths of the faith. They lived exemplary lives in the power of the Spirit, and so spread the gospel of salvation to countless others. Granted, Lois and Eunice aren't mentioned many times in Scripture, but what is said is worth Timothy's weight in heaven.

I consider it an honor and a privilege to have Thom's mother living so close to us and our children. From piano lessons to leisurely talks, we have gained so much wisdom from her lifelong experiences and have been touched by her unconditional love that we know the Lord more deeply because of her. It encourages me to know that, years from now when our kids are grown, her legacy of love will live on in them and will shine Christ's light onto generations that her eyes will only see in Glory.

Father,

I have been afraid of feeling alone and finding my purpose once the children are gone. But as it has always been, my hope is hidden in Your faithful friendship and Your call for me to help others find You, too. Give me strength to persevere to the very end, to submit to Your Spirit's leading in the daily activities of my life. And as grandchildren and great-grandchildren come along, please continue Your grace in my life to love them well and lead them to You.

Heart Reflections

BUILDING FAMILIES OF FAITH

When does our duty to build
up the body of Christ end?
Why?

As your own children grow up, what are new ways you can continue to mentor young lives?

Why is it so critical that older Christians teach the younger ones?

What kind of heritage do you want to pass on to the generations after you?

Prayer Requests

People, events, or situations
you want to pray for

Praise Reports

Record evidences of answered prayer,
moments of celebration,
and times of blessing in your life
and the world around you.

Favorite Verses

Record your favorite scriptures
and perhaps a reason why
they are so special to you.

Favorite Hymns and Christian Songs

List some of the special hymns
or songs that have touched your heart.

Spiritual Influences

Commemorate those people,
moments, or events that have
impacted your life.

Special Memories

Celebrate those memorable times
in your life by recording them here.